small bites

small bites

tapas, sushi, mezze, antipasti, and other finger foods

Jennifer Joyce

LONDON, NEW YORK, MELBOURNE, MUNICH, DELHI

This book is dedicated to Deidre, my lovely sister

Project Editor Jennifer Lane
Project Art Editor Sara Robin
Designer Andrew Barron
Senior Editor Jennifer Jones
Managing Editors Stephanie Farrow, Penny Warren
Managing Art Editor Marianne Markham
Publishing Manager Gillian Roberts
Art Director Carole Ash
Publishing Director Mary-Clare Jerram
DTP Designer Sonia Charbonnier
Production Controller Stuart Masheter
Photographer Sian Irvine

First published in Great Britain in 2005
by Dorling Kindersley Limited
80 Strand, London WC2R 0RL
Penguin Group (UK)

A CIP catalogue record for this book is available from The British Library

ISBN 1 4053 1073 1

Reproduced by Colourscan (Singapore)
Printed and bound by South China Printing Co. Ltd (China)

Discover more at
www.dk.com

Contents

Introduction

There's a revolution going on. The formality of the dining room table is being exchanged for a more relaxed gathering around the coffee table as the new mode for entertaining. Growing numbers of home cooks are unashamedly offering guests simply a selection of canapés and starters as a main meal. They are dismissing the classic three courses scenario, with large cuts of meat or fish, in favour of diminutive, yet beguiling bites.

Depending on where you happen to be, these little dishes may be called tapas, mezze, antipasti, or Asian street fare. But no matter what their origin, they share a tantalising similarity – an amalgamation of salty, sweet, sour, and spicy flavours. Once our palates are woken with such tastes, we can't help but crave more.

Delicious taste is not the only reason for this coffee table movement, however; the other is lifestyle. An evening spent surrounded by a myriad of exotic dishes promotes a more sociable, relaxed atmosphere than when plodding through multiple, formal courses. This especially suits those who want to entertain stylishly, but live in small spaces and without a dining table. The growing popularity of book clubs, girls' nights, and casual gatherings of friends are starting to change the way we entertain and cook.

Small Bites is an inspirational book that takes glorious licence in experimenting with bold tastes, such as chillies, spices, garlic, salty anchovies, and fresh herbs. People are now travelling further afield and more frequently and want to recreate their newly discovered tastes at home and with ease. As a teacher of popular

Chunky chopped salad with red wine and caper vinaigrette *(see p74)*

Crab and gruyére nachos with charred tomato salsa *(see p142)*

classes on modern ethnic cuisines such as Moorish, Middle Eastern, Pacific, and Southeast Asian cooking, I have a keen understanding of how to create exotic starters that are the most delicious and novel parts of a meal. Don't fear any ingredients that are new to you – there are useful websites (*see p223*) to help you.

To answer the needs of home cooks at all levels, the recipes offer comprehensive advice for think-ahead preparation along with suggestions for accompaniments that will balance both flavour and time involved. Inventive menu plans and cocktail ideas that suit a theme of a specific cuisine, such as Japanese or Mediterranean, are scattered throughout the book to inspire you. On these pages I have created a timeline to help you plan out the preparation.

Since some dishes are more labour intensive than others, there are six quick recipe features offering suggestions for simple dishes. Use these to add complementory recipes to your menu without placing an unrealistic demand on your time.

Peking seared duck rolls with plum sauce
(see p180)

Raspberry meringues with white chocolate swirls
(see p208)

This book is a gathering of my favourite recipes that are innovative, approachable, and most importantly have the "wow factor". I hope you enjoy making them as much as I did creating them. Whether you select dishes solely as starters or create an entire menu from them, you will not fail to impress or delight your friends.

Jennifer Joyce

Sizzling, golden, and mouthwateringly crisp – when fried food beckons, it is impossible to show restraint. Creamy dips or sticky chilli sauces add to the taste experience. This tempting, rich food is set apart from everyday fare and perfect for special occasions. Think of these tasty morsels as treats to be savoured, without remorse.

Fried

Fried artichokes Roman style
with saffron aioli

These artichokes resemble exotic flowers after they're fried, and they are as good to eat as they are to look at. Use baby ones, seasonal in spring and autumn, since they'll require far less time to prepare than their larger globe counterparts.

1 Fill a medium-sized bowl with water and add the lemon juice. Pull the tough outer leaves from the artichokes until you reach the pale tender leaves inside. Trim the stems back to 5cm (2in). Using a carrot peeler, peel the sides and ends of the stems. Using a melon baller, scoop out the fuzzy choke inside the artichokes and discard. Place the artichokes in the water to prevent discolouring.

2 Preheat the oven to 150°C (300°F/Gas mark 2). Heat a wok or small, heavy-based saucepan. Add the oil and heat until a small cube of bread, when dropped in, sizzles immediately. Remove three artichokes from the water, drain on kitchen towel, and flatten the tops by pressing them face-down on the countertop. Lower into the wok or pan, fry until golden, and drain on kitchen towel. Keep warm in the oven while you fry the remaining artichokes. Serve sprinkled with salt and accompanied by the saffron aioli.

Prepare ahead

The aioli can be made the night before and refrigerated. The artichokes can be peeled the night before, kept in the lemon water and refrigerated. They can then be fried up to 30 minutes before and kept warm in a preheated oven at 150°C (300°F/Gas mark 2).

INGREDIENTS

Juice of 2 lemons

20 baby artichokes

400ml (14fl oz) groundnut or vegetable oil

1 tsp salt

1 recipe saffron aioli (see p217), to serve

Preparation time 40 minutes
Makes 20 pieces

BUY AND ARRANGE

Baby prawns with rocket (see p149) • roasted garlic with warm bread (see p71) • chocolate hazelnut spread on toasted brioche (see p214)

PARTNER WITH

Wild mushroom crostini (see p153) • seared beef carpacico (see p128) • rosemary lamb chops (see p118) • strawberries and figs (see p207)

Coconut prawns
with mango mint dipping sauce

This tangy combination provides a fresh blend of flavours and works well for a menu based on Middle Eastern, Indian, or Pacific themes. The prawns can also be teamed successfully with other dips (*see p216–19*).

1 Preheat the oven to 150°C (300°F/Gas mark 2). Wash and dry the prawns on kitchen towel. Put the cornflour, beaten egg whites, and coconut in three separate bowls. Season the prawns with salt and pepper, then dip into the cornflour. Shake off the excess, then dip into the egg white, and finally into the coconut.

2 Heat the oil in a large wok or heavy, medium-sized saucepan, until a small piece of bread, when dropped in, sizzles immediately.

3 Deep-fry the prawns in the oil until golden, about 6 at a time. Drain on kitchen paper and keep warm in the oven until ready to serve. Accompany with the mango mint dipping sauce and garnish with lime zest, if liked.

Prepare ahead

The prawns can be coated 1 hour before frying, and kept in the refrigerator. They can be fried and kept warm in a preheated oven at 150°C (300°F/Gas mark 2) 30 minutes before serving.

INGREDIENTS

500g (1lb) medium-sized or large prawns, peeled and de-veined

125g (4oz) cornflour

4 egg whites, lightly beaten

125g (4oz) unsweetened desiccated coconut

Salt and pepper

600ml (1 pint) peanut or vegetable oil

1 recipe mango mint dipping sauce (*see p216*)

Zest of 1 lime, for garnish (*optional*)

Preparation time 35 minutes

Makes 20 large or 30 medium prawns, depending on size

BUY AND ARRANGE

Crab and cream cheese dip (*see p71*) • mango fool (*see p215*)• freshly sliced watermelon (*see p215*)

PARTNER WITH

Seared cinnamon duck (*see p124*) • red curry pumpkin soup (*see p46*) • raspberry meringues (*see p208*)

Colours

- Vivid turquoise
- Lime green
- Berry red
- Lemon yellow
- Hot pink

Tableware

- Bubble glass plates
- Strings of fairy lights
- Hand-painted plates
- Multi-coloured tablecloths
- Rainbow-striped napkins

Latin fiesta

Celebratory in spirit but relaxed in presentation, Latin food invites warm and generous entertaining. Spicy, sour, and sometimes sweet, the flavours of this cuisine are complex yet unfussy. Creamy avocados, smoky chillies, and sour limes are a few of its iconic ingredients.

No other cuisine in the world uses as many dried and fresh chillies, each with its own particular characteristics. Some have a wine-fruity taste, others are smoky, tobacco-like, or chocolatey. If I had to choose a favourite chilli, it would be the chipotle - a jalapeño that is smoked during drying and then reconstituted in a garlicky tomato sauce. This pepper adds magic smokiness to salsas, marinades, or dips. Find a good on-line supplier (*see Useful Addresses p223*) and buy a few tins of them at a time to keep your home stocked.

Think colourful and festive when preparing the table for a Latin evening. Bubble glass crockery is a Mexican classic, in blues and greens. Use any hand-painted plates you may have, especially those with vivid, colourful designs. A good assortment of brightly-coloured linens will help set the tone. Home-made salty margaritas are compulsory for this feast.

Flavours

- Chillies - fresh and dried
- Cool sour cream
- Sharp limes
- Creamy avocados
- Garlicky sauces and salsas

Nibbles

- Warm spicy almonds (*see p30*)
- Salsa with tortilla chips (*see p70*)
- Pan-fried padron peppers (*see p30*)
- Escabeche of carrots (*see p216*)
- Marinated black olives (*see p30*)

Menu

Chilli gazpacho
with sourdough croûtons

Grilled butterflied prawns
with butter, lime, and jalepeño

Crispy chorizo quesadillas
with guacamole

Soft shell steak tacos
with smoky tomatillo salsa

Serrano-rolled asparagus
with saffron aioli

Chocolate crinkle cookies
with walnuts

BUY AND ARRANGE

Watermelon and feta salad
(*see p93*)

Pan-fried padron peppers
(*see p30*)

Warm spicy almonds
(*see p30*)

Chilli gazpacho
(*see p36*)

Grilled butterflied prawns
(*see p141*)

Crispy chorizo quesadillas
(*see p186*)

Soft shell steak tacos
(*see p178*)

Serrano-rolled asparagus
(*see p152*)

Chocolate crinkle cookies
(*see p204*)

Two days before
- Make carrot escabeche
- Make chocolate cookies

The night before
- Make gazpacho and croûtons but keep separate
- Clean and butterfly prawns
- Make saffron aioli
- Make tomatillo salsa
- Marinate steaks for tacos

In the morning
- Squeeze limes for margaritas
- Chop ingredients for grilled butterflied prawns
- Make guacamole
- Make Serrano-rolled asparagus

Classic margarita

Buy a tequila that is 100% agave, if you can. This ensures quality and will minimise the risk of a headache the next day.

INGREDIENTS

Coarse salt

1 lime, cut into wedges

250ml (8fl oz) 100% agave tequila

250ml (8fl oz) orange liqueur, such as Cointreau

250ml (8fl oz) fresh lime juice

5 tbsp sugar

1 large handful of ice

Makes 8 generous margaritas

Scatter salt onto a plate. Rub the rims of each glass with the lime wedges then dip each into the salt to coat. Pour the remaining ingredients into a blender or cocktail shaker, and blend or shake well. Pour into glasses and add more ice to the glasses if desired.

One hour before
- Assemble quesadillas; leave uncooked
- Grill onions for tacos
- Blend or shake margaritas
- Pour gazpacho into cups; refrigerate
- Make watermelon salad; keep dressing separate

Half an hour before
- Cook quesadillas
- Grill steaks for tacos
- Cook padron peppers; plate
- Plate chocolate cookies
- Pan-fry almonds; plate
- Plate Serrano-rolled asparagus

At the last minute
- Blend margaritas again; pour
- Grill butterflied prawns; plate
- Plate quesadillas
- Plate steak tacos
- Plate watermelon salad with dressing
- Serve gazpacho with croûtons

Crispy vegetable pakoras
with tamarind and ginger dipping sauce

Pakoras are one of the few fried snacks you can prepare well in advance and will retain their crunchy coating. Gram flour can be found in the Indian section of most supermarkets (*see useful addresses p223*).

1 Preheat the oven to 200°C (400°F/Gas mark 6). Combine the flours, spices, and salt with the water, and beat to a smooth batter. The mixture should be thick, so add additional flour if necessary.

2 Pour the oil into a thick, heavy-based, medium-sized saucepan or large wok that will maintain the heat level. Heat until a small piece of bread, when dropped in, sizzles immediately.

3 Dip the vegetable pieces into the batter one at a time, then drop into the hot oil. Deep-fry up to 6 pieces at a time, but don't overcrowd the saucepan. Cook for 3–4 minutes, until golden. Remove from the oil with a slotted spoon, and drain on kitchen towel. Keep warm in the oven until ready to serve. Garnish with the mint and serve with the tamarind and ginger dipping sauce.

Prepare ahead

The pakoras can be fried up to 4 hours ahead, kept at room temperature, and then reheated for 5 minutes in an oven preheated to 200°C (400°F/Gas mark 6). The sauce can be made up to 3 days ahead and refrigerated.

INGREDIENTS

30g (1oz) gram flour, plus extra if necessary (*see method*)

45g (1½oz) self-raising flour

½ tsp garam masala

¼ tsp ground cumin

¼ tsp ground turmeric

¼ tsp chilli powder

½ tsp salt

150ml (5fl oz) water

1 litre (1¾ pints) groundnut or vegetable oil

25 very thin slices of any of these vegetables: onion, potato, aubergine, baby artichoke, green beans, or fennel

Tamarind and ginger dipping sauce (*see p219*), to serve

Mint sprigs, to garnish

Preparation time 15 minutes
Cooking time 15 minutes
Makes around 25 pieces

BUY AND ARRANGE	PARTNER WITH
Tomato and coconut sambal (*see p92*) • selection of chutneys and pickles (*see p70*) • Indian sugar-coated fennel seeds (*see p215*)	Halibut parcels (*see p146*) • tomato and ginger soup (*see p50*) • raspberry meringues (*see p208*)

Mozzarella en carrozza
with capers

A grilled cheese sandwich seems uninspired next to these tastey little bites from Naples. Sourdough or campagne bread may not be authentic, but will ensure every bite is chewy.

1   Cut the mozzarella into 1cm (½in) thick slices. Divide evenly between the 5 slices of bread. Sprinkle with the capers and top with the remaining bread. Slice the crusts off the sandwiches.

2   In a bowl, beat together the eggs, milk, salt, and pepper. Heat the butter and olive oil in a non-stick sauté pan over a medium low heat. Dip the sandwiches, two at a time, into the egg mixture. Fry for about 2 minutes on each side, until golden, then drain on kitchen towel. Cut into quarters and serve.

Prepare ahead
The egg mixture can be prepared 3 hours ahead and refrigerated. The sandwiches can be fried and kept warm in a preheated oven at 160°C (325°F/Gas mark 3) for 30 minutes before serving.

INGREDIENTS

500g (1lb) fresh mozzarella, drained and at room temperature

10 thin slices sourdough or campagne bread

1 tbsp small capers, rinsed

2 large eggs, beaten

60ml (2fl oz) milk

1 tsp salt

½ tsp black pepper

15g (½oz) butter

1 tbsp olive oil

Preparation time 15 minutes
Cooking time 20 minutes
Makes 20 sandwiches

BUY AND ARRANGE

Pan-fried chorizo (*see p149*) • marinated anchovies (*see p30*) • fig, proscuitto, and mozzarella salad (*see p92*)

PARTNER WITH

Bagna cauda dip (*see p54*) • farro salad (*see p78*) • artichoke puff pastry bites (*see p196*)

Chunky aubergine sticks
with Parmesan

Uncomplicated yet utterly addictive, these plump aubergine sticks are pre-soaked in water to keep them crispy yet still full and juicy once fried.

1 Place the aubergine sticks in a large bowl of cold water and soak for 1 hour. Heat the olive oil in a wok or medium-sized, heavy-based saucepan. It will be hot enough when a small piece of aubergine, when dropped in, sizzles immediately.

2 Spread the flour on a plate. Lift the aubergine sticks from the water, dip into the flour to coat, then shake off the excess. Fry 4–6 sticks at a time, until golden brown, and drain on kitchen paper. Sprinkle with the salt, pepper, and Parmesan. Serve with the lemon wedges.

Prepare ahead

The aubergines can be fried and kept in a preheated oven at 160°C (325°F/Gas mark 3) for 30 minutes before serving.

INGREDIENTS

2 large aubergines, trimmed and cut into 2cm (¾in) sticks

350ml (12fl oz) vegetable oil

125g (4oz) plain flour

1 tsp each salt and pepper

6 tbsp Parmesan, finely grated

Lemon wedges, to serve

Preparation time 5 minutes, plus 1 hour soaking
Cooking time 15 minutes
Makes 20–30 sticks

BUY AND ARRANGE

Radicchio, orange, and rocket salad (*see p92*) • marinated olives (*see p30*) • biscotti, mascarpone, and dessert wine (*see p215*)

PARTNER WITH

Baby clams (*see p136*) • bresaola and pear rolls (*see p188*) • chocolate Frangelico pudding (*see p200*)

Crispy scallops
with wasabi mayonnaise

These sweet scallops are light, versatile, and work well with most sauces, so use your imagination (*see pp216–19*). Instead of ordinary breadcrumbs, try the panko variety. They can be found in Asian and gourmet food shops.

1 Season the scallops with the salt and pepper. Put the eggs, flour, and breadcrumbs in three separate bowls. Dip the scallops in the flour. Shake off the excess, then dip in the egg, and finally in the breadcrumbs. Keep refrigerated until ready to fry.

2 Heat a wok or small, heavy-based saucepan. Pour in the oil and heat until a breadcrumb, when dropped in, sizzles immediately. Deep-fry the scallops, about three to four at a time, until golden. Drain on kitchen towel. Slice the spring onion into fine julienne and curl with the edge of a knife. Serve the cakes warm, garnished with spring onion curls and lime wedges, and accompanied by the wasabi.

Prepare ahead

The scallops can be coated and sauces prepared on the morning of serving and stored in the refrigerator.

INGREDIENTS

20 medium-sized or large scallops, with corals removed

½ tsp each salt and pepper

2 eggs, beaten

125g (4oz) plain flour

125g (4oz) toasted breadcrumbs or panko breadcrumbs

400ml (14fl oz) groundnut or vegetable oil

Spring onion, to garnish

Lime wedges, to serve

1 recipe wasabi mayonnaise (*see p219*) and/or ponzu soy dipping sauce (*see p217*)

Preparation time 35 minutes

Makes 20 pieces

BUY AND ARRANGE

Roasted asparagus with soy (*see p172*) • watercress salad with spring onion (*see p93*) • selection of sushi (*see p31*)

PARTNER WITH

Sticky chicken wings (*see p126*) • roasted butternut squash (*see p163*) • coconut macaroons (*see p210*)

Thai sweetcorn fritters
with sweet chilli and coriander sauce

The quintessential late-summer vegetable, sweetcorn kernels cut fresh from the cob have an intense flavour. Self-raising flour is the secret to making these fritters fluffy and light.

1 Cut the kernels from the cobs and place them in a medium-sized bowl. Stir in both types of flour, the chilli powder, spring onions, salt, and pepper. Gradually beat in the beer to form a batter. Mix well and leave to rest for at least 30 minutes.

2 Pour the oil into a thick, heavy-based, medium-sized saucepan or large wok. Heat until a small piece of bread, when dropped in, sizzles instantly. Drop in the batter, 1 tablespoon at a time, and fry the fritters in batches of about 6 for around 5 minutes, until golden and crispy. Drain on kitchen towel. Garnish with the coriander and serve hot with the sauce.

Prepare ahead

The batter can be prepared 3 hours in advance and refrigerated. The sweet chilli sauce can be made 2 days ahead and refrigerated. Alternatively, the fritters may be fried and frozen, then thawed in the refrigerator and baked for 5 minutes in an oven preheated to 200°C (400°F/Gas mark 6).

INGREDIENTS

5 fresh corn cobs

125g (4oz) plain flour

60g (2oz) self-raising flour

1 tsp chilli powder

4 spring onions, finely sliced

½ tsp each salt and pepper

250ml (8fl oz) beer

450ml (15fl oz) vegetable or groundnut oil

Coriander sprigs, to garnish

1 recipe sweet chilli and coriander sauce (see p218) or bottled sweet chilli dipping sauce, to serve

Preparation time 10 minutes
Cooking time 30 minutes
Makes 24 fritters

BUY AND ARRANGE

Crab and cream cheese dip (see p71) • selection of sushi (see p31) • fresh unpeeled lychees (see p215)

PARTNER WITH

Seared duck and mango salad (see p90) • five spice hoisin ribs (see p132) • passion fruit trifle (see p206)

Ithaca courgette cakes
with dill yoghurt sauce

The breadcrumbs keep these vegetable cakes plump and crisp. The cakes are equally tempting hot or at room temperature, with the refreshing dill yoghurt for dipping.

1 To remove the excess moisture from the courgettes, grate, sprinkle with the salt, and leave in a colander for 30 minutes. Meanwhile, preheat the oven to 190°C (375°F/Gas mark 5). Reserve 8 tablespoons of breadcrumbs, spread the remaining breadcrumbs on a non-stick baking sheet, and bake for 10 minutes, stirring a couple of times, until golden and crisp. Set aside to cool.

2 Rinse the courgettes and squeeze with your hands to remove as much liquid as possible, or the cakes will be too wet. Spread on a clean tea towel and blot with another. Mix the courgettes with the onions, eggs, feta, reserved breadcrumbs, mint, and nutmeg, and season. Using floured hands, form the mixture into 15–18 plump, round 5cm (2in) wide patties. Press the patties into the breadcrumbs, enusuring that they are coated all over.

3 Heat a frying pan over a medium high heat. Add enough olive oil to submerge half of each pattie, and heat until a small piece of bread, dropped in, sizzles immediately. Fry the patties for about 3 minutes on each side, until crisp and golden. Drain on kitchen towel. Serve with the yoghurt sauce and lemon wedges.

Prepare ahead

The cakes can be fried 2 hours before serving and reheated for 5 minutes in an oven preheated to 200°C (400°F/Gas mark 6). The dill yoghurt sauce can be prepared on the morning of serving.

INGREDIENTS

500g (1lb) small courgettes, topped and tailed

1 tbsp salt

175g (6oz) fine fresh breadcrumbs

6 spring onions, finely chopped

2 eggs, lightly beaten

100g (3½oz) feta cheese, crumbled

40g (1½oz) fresh mint, chopped

¼ tsp nutmeg

A little flour, for shaping (*see method*)

Olive oil, for frying

1 recipe dill yoghurt sauce (*see p216*), to serve

Lemon wedges, to serve

Preparation time 30 minutes
Cooking time 12 minutes
Makes 15–18 small cakes

BUY AND ARRANGE

Tomato and feta skewers (*see p31*) • Middle Eastern pastries (*see p214*) • frisée with quail's eggs (*see p93*)

PARTNER WITH

Roasted prawns and tomatoes (*see p145*) • beetroot pesto (*see p67*) • chunky chopped salad (*see p74*)

Quick nibbles
buy and arrange ideas for quick-to-prepare snacks

These quick nibbles are perfect to serve at the beginning of the evening while your guests are arriving. The recipes are devilishly moreish, especially the caramelized nuts and crostinis. Choose your nibbles according to the theme of the evening, how much time you have left to prepare food, and the drinks you are serving.

Marinated olives

There are two olive recipes, with both, leave to marinate for 30 minutes to an hour, then serve. Olive mix 1: mix together 2 handfuls of good-quality, large, pitted green olives, 2 finely chopped tender stalks of celery, 1 teaspoon fennel seeds, and 1 garlic clove, finely sliced. Olive mix 2: mix together 2 handfuls of good-quality, pitted black olives, 2 strips of orange zest, 1 garlic clove, crushed, and 1 teaspoon dried oregano.

Pan-fried padron peppers

Heat 1 tablespoon olive oil in a non-stick frying pan until hot and pan-fry 3–4 handfuls of small sweet green peppers, such as padrons, for about 4 minutes. Shake the pan regularly to prevent sticking. Serve on small plates, sprinkled with flaked sea salt.

Marinated anchovies

Buy about 125g (4oz) fresh anchovies, and place them in a serving dish. Drizzle over 1 teaspoon red wine vinegar and 1 tablespoon extra virgin olive oil. Sprinkle with 1 tablespoon freshly chopped parsley, then season.

Caramelized nuts

In a baking try, mix 2 large handfuls of nuts, such as pecans, hazelnuts, or walnuts, with 4 tablespoons maple syrup, 2 tablespoons sugar, ½ teaspoon cayenne pepper, and 1 tablespoon extra virgin olive oil. Bake for 10 minutes at 180°C (350°F/Gas mark 4) then allow to cool on a non-stick surface. To create an Asian flavour, add 1 teaspoon soy sauce.

Spanish or Italian deli plate

Visit your local delicatessen or supermarket in search of special foods to create either a Spanish or Italian theme. Look for items such as pickled garlic, breads and breadsticks, marinated artichoke hearts, olives, pepperincini, salted almonds, interesting cheeses, salamis, and air-dried hams, such as Serrano or prosciutto. Serve them presented on a platter.

Warm spicy almonds

Put 125g (4oz) Spanish or another variety of whole blanched almonds in a frying pan with 1 tablespoon olive oil and 1 teaspoon smoky paprika or chilli powder. Pan-fry until completely golden. Serve immediately in small bowls.

Tomato and feta skewers

To make 20 skewers, cut a piece of feta into
2.5cm (1in) cubes and chop 10 cherry tomatoes
in half. Feed 1 cube of feta and a tomato half
onto each skewer. In a bowl, mix 1 teaspoon
crushed fennel seeds, 1 tablespoon grated
lemon rind, a pinch of crushed chillis, and
1 tablespoon extra virgin olive oil. Place the
skewers in a dish, season, pour over the
marinade mixture and leave for an hour. Serve
the skewers on a platter.

Selection of sushi

Visit your local supermarket or a specialist shop
and buy the freshest sushi available. Serve the
selection of fish and rolls with chopsticks,
wasabi paste, soy dipping sauce, and perhaps
a few glasses of sake.

Gorgonzola crostini with red onion

Toast some sliced sourdough or French bread,
then spread a thick slice of gorgonzola over
each slice. Top with a couple thinly sliced rings
of red onion and a sprinkling of balsamic vinegar.
Season with black pepper and serve.

Pistachios or Japanese rice-coated peanuts

Visit your local supermarket or a specialist shop
to buy fresh, unshelled pistachios, Japanese
rice-coated peanuts, or any other of your
favourite nuts, and serve them in small bowls.

Prosciutto-wrapped melon

Prosciutto-wrapped melon

Cut a cantaloupe, or any other sweet melon,
into 2.5cm (1in) chunks. Slice some prosciutto,
or Serrano ham, into small strips. Wrap a strip
of ham around each chunk of melon and secure
it a with toothpick or skewer.

Parmesan crisps

Freshly grate some parmesan and arrange it in
thin piles, about 2 tablespoons at a time, on a
baking sheet lined with non-stick paper. Bake
for 7 minutes at 200°C (400°F/Gas mark 6).
Remove from the oven and let it sit for 1 minute
then transfer with a fish slice to a cooling rack.

Steaming hot or refreshingly chilled, soups offer comfort and joy. They are an excellent showcase for the many delicious vegetables and aromatic herbs and spices on offer. Don't be shy with embellishments: croûtons, dumplings, and pomegranate seeds can be savoured with each mouthful.

Soups

Creamy celery and fennel soup
with chilled grapes

This is a wonderfully refreshing and satisfying soup. The sweet, plump grapes enliven the velvety texture with their revitalizing freshness and purple colour.

1   Heat the butter and olive oil in a large saucepan over medium heat. Add the fennel, onion, celery, fennel seed, celery seed, and garlic. Season and sauté, stirring occasionally, for about 10 minutes, until softened. Add the white wine, lemon juice, and stock and simmer for 20 minutes. Stir in the cream and continue to cook gently for a further 5 minutes.

2   Pour the mixture into a blender or food processor and purée. Serve it in small cups, teacups, or small glasses, garnished with grapes and chives.

Prepare ahead

The soup can be made 2 days in advance, covered, refrigerated, and reheated before serving. Alternatively, it may be frozen for up to 4 weeks.

INGREDIENTS

1 tbsp butter

2 tbsp olive oil

2 fennel bulbs, cored, sliced and chopped

1 medium-sized yellow onion, finely chopped

1 celery heart, sliced

½ tsp fennel seeds, crushed

¼ tsp celery seed

2 garlic cloves, finely chopped

½ tsp each salt and pepper

175ml (6fl oz) white wine

Juice of ½ lemon

400m (14fl oz) chicken or vegetable stock

60ml (2fl oz) single cream

1 large handful purple seedless grapes, halved

Chopped chives, to garnish (*optional*)

Preparation time 25 minutes
Cooking time 35 minutes
Makes 8 small cups or 4 bowls

BUY AND ARRANGE	PARTNER WITH
Frisée with quail's eggs (*see p93*) • smoked salmon blinis (*see p148*) • lemon curd spread on toasted brioche (*see p214*)	Baby beetroot and bresaola (*see p168*) • seared beef carpaccio (*see p128*) • baby clams (*see p136*)

Chilli gazpacho
with sourdough croûtons

Nothing is as easy, healthy, and refreshing as gazpacho.
If you can't find an ancho chilli, use any other dried red chilli
or a teaspoon of Tabasco sauce.

1 Soak the ancho chilli in boiling water for 15 minutes. Drain,
place in the food processor or blender with the water and purée.
Reserve 1 tablespoon of the mixture and transfer the rest to a jar.
Float a little oil over the top to cover, and seal the jar. Store the jar
for use another time.

2 Place the tomatoes, onion, cucumber, and peppers in a large
bowl. Add the ancho chilli purée, garlic, bread, olive oil, stock,
vinegar, spices, salt, and pepper. Stir to combine thoroughly.
Transfer to a food processor or blender and process to a smooth
purée. If you want a finer texture, sieve the mixture. Chill for at
least 4 hours or overnight.

3 Divide the soup between 8 cups or 4 bowls, top with the
sourdough croûtons, and serve cold.

Prepare ahead

The soup can be made the night before, and tastes much better
if you do so.

INGREDIENTS

1 dried ancho chilli, de-seeded
and stem removed

2 tbsp water

3 tbsp olive oil, plus a little to
top the purée

500g (1lb) ripe plum tomatoes,
coarsely chopped

1 small red onion, coarsely
chopped

1 small cucumber, coarsely
chopped

½ large red pepper, de-seeded
and coarsely chopped

½ yellow pepper, de-seeded
and coarsely chopped

1 garlic clove, crushed

2 slices white bread, crusts
removed and torn into chunks

250ml (8fl oz) cold chicken
stock

2 tbsp sherry vinegar

½ tsp pimenton

1 tsp cumin seed, toasted

½ tsp each salt and pepper

1 recipe sourdough croûtons
(see three tomato salad, p86),
to serve

Preparation time 25 minutes,
plus 4 hours or overnight
chilling time

Makes 8 small cups or 4 bowls

BUY AND ARRANGE	PARTNER WITH
Salsa with tortilla chips (see p70) • baby lettuce with walnut oil and sherry vinegar (see p92) • ice cream with sweet sherry (see p215)	Beef and sweet potato skewers (see p114) • crispy chorizo quesadillas (see p186) • crab and gruyére nachos (see p142)

Mushroom and chestnut soup
with truffle oil

Chestnuts have a true affinity for mushrooms. If you are feeling extravagant, drizzle over some truffle oil when ready to serve.

1 Soak the porcini mushrooms in 500ml (16fl oz) of boiling water for 15 minutes. Put the olive oil in a medium-sized saucepan, heat to medium high, and add the onion, salt, and pepper. Sauté for 4 minutes, then add the garlic. Reduce the heat to medium and sauté for 2 minutes. Add the fresh mushrooms and chestnuts, and sauté for a further minute before adding the stock.

2 Drain the porcini, reserving the liquid. Rinse, chop finely, and add to the soup. Sieve the liquid through kitchen paper to catch any additional grit or dirt, pour it into the soup, and cook for 20 minutes. Stir in the cream and lemon juice. Season to taste, then transfer to a blender and purée. Return to the saucepan to warm through. Serve in cups or bowls, garnished with chopped chives and a drizzle of truffle oil, if using.

Prepare ahead

The soup can be made 2 days before, refrigerated and reheated. It may also be frozen for up to 4 weeks.

INGREDIENTS

30g (1oz) dried porcini mushrooms

6 tbsp olive oil

1 yellow onion, finely diced

½ tsp each salt and pepper

2 garlic cloves, finely chopped

500g (1lb) of chestnut, white button, or Portobello mushrooms, stems trimmed and finely chopped

100g (3½oz) vacuum-packed chestnuts, finely chopped

600ml (1 pint) chicken or vegetable stock

125ml (4fl oz) single cream

Juice of ½ lemon

Chives, chopped, for garnish

Truffle oil, to garnish (*optional*)

Preparation time 20 minutes
Cooking time 28 minutes
Makes 8 small cups or 4 bowls

BUY AND ARRANGE	PARTNER WITH
Shaved celery salad (*see p92*) • white bean dip (*see p71*) • ice cream with sweet sherry (*see p214*)	Spiced goat's cheese balls (*see p59*) • spinach and peppered pear salad (*see p84*) • roasted prawns and tomatoes (*see p145*)

Orange and beetroot soup
with iced yoghurt cubes

This colourful soup will win over anyone with a beetroot aversion. If you haven't pre-made the ice cubes, simply stir in a spoonful of yoghurt before serving.

1 Put the yoghurt in a bowl and stir in half of the chives. Spoon the mixture into an ice-cube tray and place in the freezer until frozen.

2 Put the beetroot in a saucepan, cover with water, and boil for 45 minutes to 1 hour, or until easily pierced with a knife. When cool enough to handle, remove the skins, chop roughly, and set aside.

3 Meanwhile, heat the olive oil in a medium-sized saucepan and add the onion, garlic, thyme, salt, and pepper. Sauté for 10 minutes, then add the beetroot, vinegar, orange juice, zest, and stock. Simmer for 10 minutes, then transfer to a blender or food processor and purée.

4 Stir in the cream and taste for seasoning. Transfer to cups or bowls, drop in the iced yoghurt cubes, and sprinkle with the remaining chives.

Prepare ahead

The soup can be made the day before and refrigerated, or frozen for up to 3 weeks.

INGREDIENTS

200g (7oz) plain yoghurt

Small bunch of chives, chopped

500g (1lb) small beetroot, scrubbed and leaves trimmed

6 tbsp olive oil

1 onion, chopped

2 garlic cloves, finely chopped

1 tbsp chopped fresh thyme

½ tsp each salt and pepper

1 tsp balsamic vinegar

Juice of ½ orange

1 tbsp grated orange zest

1 litre (1¾ pints) chicken or vegetable stock

3 tbsp single cream

Preparation time 15 minutes
Cooking time 1 hour
Makes 8 small cups or 4 bowls

BUY AND ARRANGE

Prosciutto-wrapped melon (*see p31*) • crushed feta dip (*see p70*) • roasted new potatoes with smoky paprika (*see p173*)

PARTNER WITH

Pan-fried halloumi salad (*see p82*) • smoky aubergine purée (*see p64*) • fried artichokes Roman style (*see p12*)

Saffron coconut soup
with prawn dumplings

Tom yum paste is made from ingredients such as galangal, lemongrass, chilli, garlic, and lime and it honestly tastes better than any homemade version.

1 To make the dumplings, place the ginger, garlic, shallots, and coriander in a food processor and process until finely chopped. Add the prawns, egg white, cornflour, and seasoning, and process to combine thoroughly. Rub oil over your hands to prevent sticking, and roll the mixture into 1cm (½in) meatballs. Set aside and refrigerate.

2 Place the coconut milk in a medium-sized saucepan and heat gently. Add the tom yum paste, lime juice, and saffron, stir well, bring to a gentle boil, then reduce the heat. Just before serving, add the dumplings and watercress. As soon as the dumplings float to the top, remove from the soup from the heat and pour into cups, glasses, or teacups. Sprinkle with coriander and serve.

Prepare ahead

The soup can be made the day before and refrigerated. The dumplings can be prepared on the morning of serving, then covered and refrigerated. Alternatively, make them up to 2 weeks ahead, place in an airtight container, and freeze.

INGREDIENTS

2 x 400ml (14fl oz) cans coconut milk

1 tbsp instant tom yum paste or 1 tom yum stock cube

Juice of ½ lime

Small pinch saffron threads, crushed

1 large bunch watercress, roughly chopped

Small handful fresh coriander, to garnish

Dumplings

1 tsp grated fresh root ginger

½ garlic clove, chopped

2 shallots, sliced

1 tsp fresh chopped coriander

200g (7oz) raw peeled prawns

1 egg white

1 tsp cornflour

¼ tsp each salt and pepper

Olive oil, for shaping (see method)

Preparation time 15 minutes
Cooking time 10 minutes
Makes 8 small servings

BUY AND ARRANGE	PARTNER WITH
Selection of sushi (see p31) • Japanese rice-coated peanuts (see p31) • fresh unpeeled lychees (see p215)	Glass noodle salad (see p76) • seafood spring rolls (see p176) • raspberry meringues (see p208)

Yellow lentil soup
with prunes, apricots, and pomegranates

Dried fruit lends depth to the lentils, and together with the pomegranate molasses makes a glorious sweet and sour soup. In summer, blend in some yoghurt and serve chilled.

1 Heat the oil in a large saucepan. Add the onions, carrots, garlic, ginger, salt, and pepper, and sauté for about 10 minutes, until soft. Add the dried fruit, cumin, cardamom, cloves, and cinnamon. Sauté for a few minutes before adding the stock. Stir in the lentils and cook, covered, for about 1 hour, until the lentils are very soft.

2 Stir in the pomegranate molasses and fresh herbs, and taste for seasoning. Serve in small cups or mugs, garnished with pomegranate seeds and coriander sprigs. If liked, the soup may be puréed for a smoother texture.

Prepare ahead

The soup may be made 2 days in advance, and refrigerated, or frozen for up to 4 weeks.

INGREDIENTS

3 tbsp olive oil

2 onions, chopped

2 carrots, finely chopped

3 garlic cloves, finely chopped

2.5cm (1in) piece ginger root, grated

½ tsp each salt and pepper

6 pitted prunes, roughly chopped

8 ready-to-eat apricots, roughly chopped

1 tsp ground cumin

¼ tsp ground cardamom

¼ tsp ground cloves

2 cinnamon sticks

1 litre (1¾ pints) chicken or vegetable stock

250g (8oz) yellow or red lentils

2 tbp pomegranate molasses or juice of 1 lemon

Small handful of mint leaves, chopped

Small handful coriander, chopped, plus sprigs to garnish

Pomegranate seeds, to garnish

Preparation time 20 minutes
Cooking time 1¼ hour
Serves 8 small cups or 4 bowls

BUY AND ARRANGE	PARTNER WITH
Lebanese salad plate (*see p93*) • houmous with smoked paprika (*see p70*) • oranges with rose water (*see p214*)	Spinach and yoghurt dip (*see p66*) • saffron chicken skewers (*see p98*) • cardamom-poached apricots (*see p211*)

Red curry pumpkin soup
with crispy fried shallots

A Thai red curry paste is very useful as a quick-fix for meals and adds real spice to this soup. The fried shallots provide a spirited counterpoint to the richness of the pumpkin.

1 Place 2 tablespoons of oil in a medium-sized saucepan, add the garlic, and fry until browned. Stir in the curry paste, fry for 3 minutes, stirring constantly, then pour in the coconut milk. Stir in the fish sauce, lime zest and juice, sugar, and stock. Simmer for 2 minutes. Reduce the heat, add the pumpkin, and cook for a further 8–10 minutes, or until soft.

2 Place the flour in a small bowl, add the shallots, and toss to coat. Remove the shallots and shake off the excess flour. Pour the remaining oil in a wok or a small, heavy-based saucepan. Heat until a small piece of bread, when dropped in, sizzles immediately. Add the shallots and fry for 1–2 minutes, until golden. Drain on kitchen towel and sprinkle with salt.

3 Serve the warm soup in cups or bowls, sprinkled with the shallots and the coriander sprigs.

Prepare ahead

The soup can be made the day before and refrigerated. If doing this, undercook the pumpkin so that it doesn't become mushy when reheated. The soup may also be frozen for up to 4 weeks. The fried shallots can be prepared 3 hours in advance and kept in an airtight container. Reheat for 5 minutes in an oven preheated to 200°C (400°F/Gas mark 6).

INGREDIENTS

600ml (1 pint) groundnut or vegetable oil, plus 2 tbsp

1 garlic clove, chopped

4 tbsp good-quality Thai red curry paste

400ml (14oz) coconut milk

1 tbsp fish sauce

Zest and juice of 1 lime

1 tbsp castor sugar

125ml (4fl oz) chicken stock

500g (1lb) pumpkin, de-seeded and cut into 2.5cm (1in) pieces

4 tbsp plain flour

5 shallots, sliced very thinly

A few sprigs of coriander, to garnish

Preparation time 10 minutes
Cooking time 18 minutes
Makes 8 small cups or 4 bowls

BUY AND ARRANGE

Watercress salad with spring onion (see p93) • prawn and cucumber skewers (see p149) • freshly sliced kiwi (see p215)

PARTNER WITH

Thai sweetcorn fritters (see p26) • crispy pork (see p119) • avocado crostini (see p164)

Meatball and pecorino soup
with caramelized onion and greens

These tiny meatballs combine with the pungent greens, caramelized onion, and sharp pecorino cheese creating a satisfying soup. Pork can easily be used in place of the veal.

1 To make the soup, heat the oil in a heavy-based, medium-sized saucepan. Add the onion, season, and sauté for about 10 minutes until the onions are golden brown and caramelized. Remove from the heat and set aside.

2 Meanwhile, bring a large saucepan of salted water to the boil. Add the chopped kale and cook for about 4 minutes, making sure it is cooked but still firm. Drain, rinse in cold water, and set aside.

3 To make the meatballs, place the bread in a medium-sized bowl, spoon the milk over to soften it, and break up the bread with your fingers. Add the remaining meatball ingredients and mix well. Using floured hands, roll the mixture into 1cm (⅓in) balls. Heat a small amount of olive oil in a non-stick frying pan, add the meatballs, and fry, turning regularly, until browned and crisp.

4 Add the kale, stock, and meatballs to the onions in the saucepan, and heat through. Ladle into cups or bowls, and sprinkle with the pecorino. Serve with some small slices of toast, if using.

Prepare ahead

The onions can be caramelized 2 days in advance. The soup may also be frozen for up to 4 weeks.

INGREDIENTS

3 tbsp olive oil

2 yellow onions, thinly sliced

200g (7oz) curly kale, chopped

700ml (1⅕ pint) chicken stock

4 tbsp pecorino cheese, shaved into slivers

Bread, toasted, to serve (*optional*)

Meatballs

1 slice white bread

2 tbsp milk

250g (8oz) minced veal or pork

½ garlic clove, finely chopped

2 tbsp Parmesan

1 egg yolk, beaten

1 tsp salt

2 tbsp flat-leaf parsley, finely chopped

Flour, to dust hands (*see method*)

1 tbsp olive oil, for frying

Preparation 20 minutes
Cooking time 20 minutes
Makes 8 small cups or 4 bowls

BUY AND ARRANGE	PARTNER WITH
Radicchio, orange, and rocket salad (*see p92*) • biscotti, mascapone, and dessert wine (*see p215*)	Serrano-rolled asparagus (*see p152*) • bagna cauda dip (*see p54*) • chocolate Frangelico pudding (*see p200*)

Tomato and ginger soup
with spiced oil

This recipe is based on a restorative soup in India called rasam that is said to be the equivalent of the comforting "chicken soup". Use the juice of two lemons instead of tamarind if necessary.

1 Place the tomatoes, garlic, and ginger in a blender or food processor, and blend for 1 minute or until smooth. Pour into a large saucepan, and add the tamarind liquid, stock, coriander, green chilli, sugar, turmeric, salt, and pepper. Bring the mixture to a boil, reduce the heat to medium, and cook for 15 minutes.

2 Meanwhile, heat the oil in a small frying pan and add the mustard seeds. When they begin to pop, add the cumin, and asafoetida, if using. Fry for 1 minute, stirring, then remove from the heat.

3 Divide the soup between 8 cups or 6 bowls. Spoon the spiced oil mixture over the top and garnish with the coriander sprigs.

Prepare ahead

The soup can be made the day before and refrigerated. Alternatively, it may be frozen for up to 4 weeks.

INGREDIENTS

15 ripe plum or vine-ripened tomatoes, chopped

6 garlic cloves

5cm (2in) piece ginger root, peeled and sliced

200ml (7fl oz) tamarind liquid or purée

200ml (7fl oz) chicken or vegetable stock

Medium-sized bunch coriander, finely chopped, plus sprigs to garnish

2 fresh green chillies, de-seeded and slit lengthways

1½ tbsp soft brown sugar

1 tsp turmeric powder

1 tsp salt

½ tsp ground black pepper

5 tbsp vegetable oil

2 tsp mustard seeds

1 tsp cumin seeds

Pinch of asafoetida (*optional*)

Preparation time 20 mins
Cooking time 20 mins
Makes 8 small cups or 6 bowls

BUY AND ARRANGE	PARTNER WITH
Selection of chutneys and pickles (*see p70*) • raita with naan bread (*see p71*) • freshly sliced watermelon (*see p215*)	Pea, prawn, and potato samosas (*see p194*) • tandoori chicken thighs (*see p130*) • chocolate cupcakes (*see p202*)

There is something beguiling about dipping; perhaps it's the absence of cutlery, the creamy textures, and the idea of sharing food with friends. From the garlicky bagna cauda and smoky black bean, to the tangy chick-pea and chilli, there is a dip here to suit every taste.

Dips

Bagna cauda dip
with crudities and quail's eggs

If you have a fondue pot, keep the bagna cauda warm in it while serving. Leave the tops of the carrots, radishes, and tomatoes untrimmed to use as natural handles.

1 To make the dip, pound the garlic and anchovies in a mortar and pestle until smooth, then transfer to a small saucepan. Add the butter and oil and simmer over heat for 4 minutes or until melted, stirring occasionally. Stir in the lemon zest and juice, parsley, and chilli. Keep warm on a very low heat until ready to serve.

2 Prepare your chosen selection of vegetables. Hard boil the eggs, if using, and peel once cooled. Serve with the dip.

Prepare ahead

The bagna cauda can be made on the morning of serving, covered and refrigerated, then gently reheated at the last minute. The vegetables can be trimmed and cut the day before, and kept in the refrigerator in an airtight container or bag.

INGREDIENTS

3 garlic cloves, finely chopped

4 large anchovies, packed in olive oil, rinsed and chopped

125g (4oz) unsalted butter

125ml (4fl oz) extra virgin olive oil

1 tsp grated lemon zest

3 tsp lemon juice

2 tbsp finely chopped flat-leaf parsley

½ tsp dried chilli, crushed

To serve

Baby carrots

Radishes

Radicchio or treviso leaves

Red pepper, thinly sliced

Cherry tomatoes on the vine

Cucumber wedges

Celery hearts with leaves, cut into batons

8 quail's eggs, boiled and peeled, served with toothpicks or skewers

Sourdough bread, toasted

Preparation time 20 minutes
Makes about 8 servings

BUY AND ARRANGE	PARTNER WITH
Spice-dusted prawns (see p148) • Italian deli plate (see p30) • marinated olives with orange (see p30)	Artichoke puff pastry bites (see p196) • sage and lemon meatballs (see p131) • three tomato salad (see p86)

Romesco dip
with roasted baby potatoes

If you can't find ancho chillis, any other large dried chilli will do. Try pimenton in place of the paprika for a smokier flavour.

1   Preheat the oven to 200°C (400°F/Gas mark 6). Place the potatoes on a large, non-stick baking sheet. Drizzle with 2 tablespoons of olive oil and sprinkle with half of the salt and pepper. Roast for 20–30 minutes, until golden and crisp. Remove and set aside.

2   Meanwhile, to make the dip, preheat the grill to high. Place the tomatoes under the grill and cook until blackened. When cool enough, remove the skins, and set aside. Place the garlic in a non-stick sauté pan and dry-fry, stirring, until blackened on all sides. Remove the skins when cool. Set aside. In the same pan, toast the almonds and hazelnuts, stirring, until golden. Set aside.

3   Put the red wine vinegar and water in a saucepan, bring to the boil, remove from the heat, and add the chillies. Soak for 10–15 minutes, until softened. Remove the peppers and discard the liquid.

4   Transfer the tomatoes, chillies, garlic, and nuts to a food processor, along with the bread, paprika, sherry vinegar, remaining olive oil, and remaining salt and pepper. Purée, leaving the nuts slightly chunky. Serve the dip with the potatoes and garnish with the flat-leaf parsley.

Prepare ahead

The dip can be prepared 2 days ahead and refrigerated. The potatoes may be slightly under-roasted 4 hours ahead, then roasted for 5–6 minutes in a oven preheated to 200°C (400°F/Gas mark 6).

INGREDIENTS

750g (1½lb) baby new potatoes

60ml (2fl oz) extra virgin olive oil, plus 2 tbsp

1 tsp each sea salt and pepper

4 large or 6 small plum tomatoes, halved

5 garlic cloves

15 almonds, skinned

15 hazelnuts, skinned

60ml (2fl oz) red wine vinegar

175ml (6fl oz) water

2 dried ancho chillies, de-seeded and stems removed

1 slice white bread, toasted

1 tsp paprika or pimenton

3 tbsp sherry vinegar

Fresh flat-leaf parsley, to garnish

Preparation time 25 minutes
Cooking time 30 minutes
Makes 8 servings

BUY AND ARRANGE

Pan-fried chorizo (*see p149*)
• tomato and feta skewers (*see p31*) • marinated fresh anchovies (*see p30*)

PARTNER WITH

Beef and sweet potato skewers (*see p114*) • Serrano-rolled asparagus (*see p152*) • courgette ribbon rolls (*see p160*)

Smoky black bean dip
with chillies and honey

This dip is incredibly healthy, so you don't have to hold back on how much you eat. Instead of the chipotle you can use another chilli or a teaspoon of Tabasco.

1 If using soaked dried beans, drain them, place in a medium-sized saucepan, and cover with water. Boil for about 45 minutes, until just tender. Drain again.

2 Meanwhile, heat the olive oil in a sauté pan. Add the onion, red pepper, chipotle pepper, and garlic. Sauté for 4 minutes. Add the beans, vinegar, honey, chilli powder, cumin, salt, and pepper. Simmer over a low heat for about 5 minutes, stirring occasionally.

3 Purée the mixture in a food processor. Add extra honey, cider vinegar, or salt, according to taste. The beans will cook and absorb flavours differently each time you prepare them. If liked, serve with salted tortilla chips and fruit salsa.

Prepare ahead
The dip can be made a week in advance and kept refrigerated.

INGREDIENTS

250g (8 oz) dried black beans, soaked overnight, or canned black beans, drained

3 tbsp olive oil

1 onion, chopped

1 red pepper, chopped

1 chipotle pepper, de-seeded and chopped

3 garlic cloves, chopped

125ml (4fl oz) cider vinegar

4 tbsp runny honey

1 tsp each chilli powder and ground cumin

1 tbsp sea salt

Freshly cracked pepper

Tortilla chips and fruit salsa (see p70), to serve (optional)

Preparation time 30 minutes
Cooking time 45 minutes
Makes about 8 servings

BUY AND ARRANGE

Watermelon and feta salad (see p93) • pan-fried chorizo (see p149) • spice-dusted prawns (see p148)

PARTNER WITH

Crab and gruyére nachos (see p142) • soft shell steak tacos (see p178) • grilled butterflied prawns (see p141)

Goat's cheese balls
rolled in spices

This dish is still impressive without the caramelized garlic, so if you are short on time make the balls with the goat's cheese and spices only.

1 To caramelize the garlic, place the cloves in a small saucepan, cover with water, and boil for 3 minutes. Drain, peel, and slice each clove into 3 pieces.

2 Heat the olive oil in a saucepan over a low heat, add the garlic and colour lightly. Drain off the oil, add the vinegar, rosemary, salt, pepper, and sugar, and cook for 3 minutes, until the liquid is reduced to a thick syrup. Pour onto a plate and leave to cool.

3 In a small bowl, mash the goat's cheese. Stir in the salt, pepper, and caramelized garlic. Mix well and roll into 2.5cm (1in) balls.

4 Place the spices in separate bowls. Roll each ball in a different spice to coat. Refrigerate for 30 minutes. Serve at room temperature with thin crackers or garlic crostini.

Prepare ahead

The cheese balls can be prepared the day before and refrigerated.

INGREDIENTS

1 small head of garlic, unpeeled

3 tbsp olive oil

2 tbsp white wine vinegar

1 tsp finely chopped rosemary

Pinch each of salt, pepper, and sugar

250g (8 oz) soft, mild rindless goat's cheese

½ tsp each salt and pepper

1 tbsp fennel seeds, crushed

1 tbsp cracked black pepper

1 tbsp crushed pink peppercorns, poppy seeds, or pimento

Thin crackers or garlic crostini, to serve

Preparation time 20 minutes
Cooking time 8 minutes
Makes about 24 balls

BUY AND ARRANGE

Chicory salad (see p93) • pesto and aioli with grissini breadsticks (see p70) • raspberry fool (see p215)

PARTNER WITH

Creamy celery and fennel soup (see p34) • chunky chopped salad (see p74) • chocolate crinkle cookies (see p204)

Colours

- Magenta pink
- Moss green
- Shimmering white
- Soft yellow
- Duck egg blue

Tableware

- Banana leaves
- Floating candles
- Straw mats
- Simple plates
- Crackle-glazed dipping bowls

Pacific feast

Follow the ring of fire that encirles the highly volcanic area around the Pacific Ocean and you will encounter China, Japan, Indonesia, Thailand, Korea, Vietnam, and Laos – all countries distinguished by lush eating. Pacific Rim cuisine has a vibrant taste characterized by lemongrass, ginger, chillies, mint, lime, and soy sauce. While this food gives the impression of being casually made, its composition is sophisticated. Texture is vitally important, providing a satisfying crunch, and each individual flavour is evident yet not dominant. Instead, there is an exquisite melange of tastes.

One of the wonderful aspects of this food is its many sauces, most featuring chillies. Some sauces are sticky, made with rice vinegar and sugar, while others comprise simply lime juice and fish sauce. Tread gently when using chillies, as you're seeking taste as well as kick. Keep in mind that the bigger the chilli, the milder its heat.

Embellish your table with a few Pacific touches – bowls filled with exotic flowers, candles floating in water, banana leaves, and straw mats. Though Pacific Rim is quintessential summer food, it's refreshing any time, even in deepest winter.

Flavours

- Tangy lime
- Fresh ginger
- Spicy chillies
- Cool mint
- Exotic lemongrass

Nibbles

- Five spice chicken bites (*see p149*)
- Crab and cream cheese dip (*see p71*)
- Rice-coated peanuts (*see p31*)
- Thai prawns (*see p149*)
- Spicy peanut dip (*see p71*)

Menu

Lemongrass beef skewers with sticky cucumber and peanut sauce

Seafood spring rolls with sweet chilli and coriander dipping sauce

Thai sweetcorn fritters with sweet chilli and coriander dipping sauce

Glass noodle salad with black pepper chicken

Peking seared duck rolls with plum sauce

Passion fruit trifle with strawberries and mascapone

BUY AND ARRANGE

Crab and cream cheese dip
(*see p71*)

Thai prawns
(*see p149*)

Rice-coated peanuts
(*see p31*)

Lemongrass beef skewers
(*see p104*)

Seafood spring rolls
(*see p176*)

Thai sweetcorn fritters
(*see p26*)

Glass noodle salad
(*see p76*)

Peking seared duck rolls
(*see p180*)

Passion fruit trifle
(*see p206*)

Two days before
- Marinate lemongrass beef
- Marinate Peking duck
- Marinate black pepper chicken
- Make sweet chilli and coriander dipping sauce

The night before
- Make seafood spring rolls
- Make passion fruit trifles

In the morning
- Assemble beef skewers
- Make sticky cucumber dipping sauce
- Grill chicken
- Sear and slice duck

Mango crush

This is a refreshing cocktail to quench your thirst while enjoying chillies, spices, and other exotic flavours. Try using watermelon or papaya in place of the mango.

INGREDIENTS

2 large ripe mangoes, peeled and chopped

Juice of 1 lime

500ml (16fl oz) freshly squeezed orange juice

2 tbsp sugar

6 measures of vodka

Ice

Mint sprigs, to garnish

Makes 6 mango crushes

Put the mango, lime and orange juice, sugar, and vodka in a food processor or blender and purée until smooth. Add some ice to 6 glasses and pour the cocktail over. Garnish with a few mint sprigs.

Two hours before
- Grill and par-cook beef skewers
- Make batter for fritters
- Make crab and cream cheese dip, ommitting the coriander and onion
- Assemble glass noodle salad, ommitting the herbs
- Make Peking duck rolls

Half to one hour before
- Fry sweetcorn fritters
- Purée mango crush
- Grill and finish cooking beef skewers, rest, then plate
- Plate seafood spring rolls with dipping sauce
- Plate Peking duck rolls

At the last minute
- Re-heat sweetcorn fritters; plate
- Toss herbs with glass noodle salad; plate
- Finish crab dip with coriander, onion, and crackers; plate
- Pour mango crush
- Serve passion fruit trifles

Smoky aubergine purée
with crushed coriander and mint

Aubergines are chameleons, changing their flavour and texture depending on the way they are cooked and the other ingredients used. Blackening them over a flame, instead of roasting, imparts a magnificent smoky taste.

1 Pierce the aubergines with a knife in several places. Using tongs, place each aubergine over an open flame on the hob. Turn each one as it blackens, and continue until it is completely charred. The insides will be fine. It can be helpful to place an old cooling rack over the flame so that you can rest the aubergine on it. Alternatively, blacken the aubergines under a grill or cook on a barbecue, but the smokiness will not be quite the same. Place in a colander to drain off any excess liquid. When cool enough to handle, carefully peel off the skin and cut off stalks.

2 While the aubergine is still warm, place the flesh in a food processor. Add the garlic, olive oil, lemon juice, yoghurt, pimenton, coriander seed, and mint, and season. Sprinkle with the chopped onion and cucumber. Serve with pitta or crudités.

Prepare ahead

The dip can be made 2 hours in advance and refrigerated, then brought to room temperature before serving. Don't add the chopped vegetables until ready to serve.

INGREDIENTS

2 large, firm aubergines

1 garlic clove, finely chopped

60ml (2fl oz) olive oil

1 tbsp fresh lemon juice

2 tbsp yoghurt

½ tsp pimenton

½ tsp coriander seeds, lightly crushed

15g (½oz) fresh mint, finely chopped

1 small red onion, finely chopped, to garnish

1 small cucumber, finely diced, to garnish

Toasted pitta or crudités, to serve

Prep time 10 minutes
Cooking time 20 minutes
Makes about 8 servings

BUY AND ARRANGE

Crushed feta dip (*see p70*) • carrots in vinaigrette (*see p173*) • Middle Eastern pastries (*see p214*)

PARTNER WITH

Serrano-wrapped prawns (*see p108*) • pan-fried halloumi salad (*see p82*) • chickpea and chilli dip (*see p68*)

Spinach and yoghurt dip
with caramelized onion

This exotic Persian dip is wondrously rich because of
the slowly caramelized onion, and the Greek yoghurt and
spinach keep it tasting fresh and healthy.

1 Place the spinach in a covered saucepan with the salt, and heat
gently for 2 minutes until it wilts. Drain and rinse with cold water,
then squeeze off any excess water with your hands until dry.

2 Place the oil in a small frying pan, add the onions and garlic,
and sauté slowly for about 20 minutes, until golden brown. It's
important to cook until caramelized to ensure the sweet flavour.
Remove from the heat, set aside, and allow to cool completely.

3 In a mixing bowl, combine the onion mixture, yoghurt, and
spinach. Season with salt and pepper. Refrigerate then serve
with warm pitta bread.

Prepare ahead

Cook the onions and spinach the morning of serving, but don't
mix with the yoghurt until 2 hours before.

INGREDIENTS

300g (11oz) fresh spinach,
chopped

1 tsp salt

2 tbsp olive oil

2 large yellow onions,
finely sliced

2 garlic cloves, crushed

200g (7oz) Greek or other
thick, full-fat yoghurt

Pitta bread, to serve

Preparation time 10 minutes
Cooking time 25 minutes
Makes about 8 servings

BUY AND ARRANGE

Piquillo peppers with sherry
vinegar (*see p172*) • baby
lettuce with walnut oil and
sherry vinegar (*see p92*)

PARTNER WITH

Saffron feta filo triangles (*see
p182*) • cardamom-poached
apricots (*see p211*) • saffron
chicken skewers (*see p98*)

Roasted beetroot pesto
with Parmesan

This is a very simple dip to make. The earthy roasted beetroot makes this pesto notable not only for its rich purple colour but also for its deliciously nutty taste.

1 Preheat the oven to 200°C (400°F/Gas mark 6). Place the beetroot on a large piece of foil, drizzle with 1 tablespoon olive oil, and season. Wrap tightly in the foil, creating an airtight package. Place in the oven for 45 minutes, or until easily pierced with a knife.

2 Remove the skin from the beetroot and discard. Put the beetroot in a food processor with the garlic, pine nuts, and ½ teaspoon salt. Purée the mixture until smooth. Add the Parmesan, purée again, then slowly add the remaining oil, still puréeing. Add extra salt, if needed. If liked, serve with garlic crostini or toasted pitta bread.

Prepare ahead

The pesto can be made 3 days in advance, covered, and kept in the refrigerator.

INGREDIENTS

2 medium-sized raw beetroot, halved

60ml (2fl oz) extra virgin olive oil, plus 1 tbsp

2 garlic cloves, peeled

100g (3½oz) pine nuts, toasted and cooled

½ tsp salt

25g (1oz) Parmesan

Garlic crostini or toasted pitta bread, to serve

Preparation time 10 minutes
Cooking time 45 minutes
Makes about 8 servings

BUY AND ARRANGE

Italian deli plate (see p30) • roasted shallots (see p173) • pan-fried chorizo (see p149)

PARTNER WITH

Fried artichokes Roman style (see p12) • farro salad (see p78) • mini peach and raspberry crisps (see p212)

Chickpea and chilli dip
with pitta crisps

Chickpeas, salty feta, and tangy pomegranate blend perfectly in this dip. One tablespoon each of lemon juice and honey mixed can be used in place of the molasses.

1 Place the chickpeas, olive oil, lemon juice, garlic, and salt in a food processor and process until just crushed. Divide between the pitta crisps or place in a serving bowl.

2 Sprinkle each pitta crisp or the bowl of dip with cumin seeds, red onion, mint, coriander, and chillies. Top with the feta cheese. Just before serving, drizzle with pomegranate molasses.

Prepare ahead

The chick-pea mixture can be puréed on the morning of serving, and the onions chopped and tossed in the lemon juice to prevent discolouring. Fresh herbs and cheese may be sprinkled on 1 hour before serving. The pitta crisps can be made 3 days ahead and stored in an airtight container.

INGREDIENTS

2 x 14oz (400g) tins of chickpeas, drained

75ml (2fl oz) extra virgin olive oil

Juice of 1 lemon

1 garlic clove, peeled and finely chopped

½ tsp salt

1 recipe pitta crisps (see p217)

1 tsp cumin seeds

1 small red onion, finely chopped

15g (½oz) fresh mint, finely chopped

15g (½oz) fresh coriander, finely chopped

2 red chillies, de-seeded and finely chopped

150g (5oz) feta cheese, crumbled

2 tbsp pomegranate molasses

Preparation time 15 minutes

Makes about 8 servings

BUY AND ARRANGE	PARTNER WITH
Pan-fried Merguez lamb sausage (see p149) • spice-dusted prawns (see p148) • Middle Eastern pastries (see p214)	Cumin lamb skewers (see p112) • Arabian salad (see p88) • strawberries and figs (see p207)

Quick dips, chutneys, and salsas
buy and arrange ideas for quick cooking

Introducing shop-bought products into your menu shouldn't make you feel as if you are cheating your guests. Instead, it can create a great base on which you can build a dish, adding your favourite spices or herbs to add a personal touch. It also allows you time to make other dishes and will leave you feeling calmer as guests arrive.

Houmous with smoked paprika

Buy a 200g (7oz) tub of houmous, tip it out onto a plate, and spread it thickly with a knife across the plate. Sprinkle over 1 teaspoon pimenton or toasted cumin seeds and drizzle with 1 teaspoon extra virgin olive oil. Serve accompanied by cos lettuce leaves or warm flat bread, such as pitta, to scoop up the dip.

Fruit salsa

Dice some fresh fruit, such as mango, papaya, or, pineapple; enough to make about 2 handfuls. Place the fruit in a bowl with 1 diced small red onion, 1 small handful chopped fresh coriander, 1 teaspoon Tabasco sauce, and the juice of 1 lime. Season and combine the mixture well. Serve with a variety of corn tortilla chips.

Pesto and aioli with grissini breadsticks, olive oil, and vinegar

Visit your local delicatessen, or the deli section of a supermarket, to buy some fresh pesto, garlic aioli, extra virgin olive oil, and balsamic vinegar. There are some interesting breadsticks available, such as grissini or sesame-coated. Pour the dips into separate bowls and serve with breadsticks.

Crushed feta dip with lemon juice and cumin

Buy a 200g (7oz) pack of feta and crumble it roughly into a bowl. Add 1 tablespoon extra virgin olive oil, ½ finely chopped small red onion, the zest and juice of 1 lemon, and ½ teaspoon toasted cumin seeds. Combine the mixture together well and serve with fresh crusty bread or carrot batons.

Selection of chutneys and pickles with mini poppadoms

Buy some jars of good-quality lime pickle and mango chutney, and seek out any other Indian-inspired pickles. Serve them in separate bowls with serving spoons and some mini poppadoms or naan bread.

Mexican salsa with tortilla chips

There are some excellent-quality Mexican salsas available in the supermarkets. Buy your favourite and if you wish to give it an extra kick, add a few drops of Tabasco sauce, a squeeze of half a lime, and a small handful of chopped fresh coriander. Stir in the added ingredients and serve with unsalted tortilla chips.

Crab and cream cheese dip

Spread 125g (4oz) cream cheese over a plate with a knife. Sprinkle over a large handful of fresh cooked or tinned white crab meat. Drizzle with 2 tablespoons sweet chilli dipping sauce and 1 small handful freshly chopped coriander. Serve with prawn crackers. Alternatively, arrange the dip on individual prawn crackers.

Roasted garlic with warm bread

Cut 2 bulbs of garlic in half, drizzle with 1 tablespoon olive oil, and wrap each half in kitchen foil. Roast them in the oven for 1 hour at 200°C (400°F/Gas mark 6). Spread the insides of the cloves with a knife onto slices of fresh bread, preferably a French baguette. Discard the skins of the cloves. Top the bread with soft goat's cheese, if desired.

Yoghurt and dill dip

In a bowl, blend together some Greek yoghurt, about 200g (7oz), with 1 crushed garlic clove, 2 chopped spring onions and a small handful of finely chopped dill. Serve with pitta or cucumber cut into batons.

Raita with naan bread

In a bowl, mix together about 200g (7oz) Greek yoghurt, 1 small diced and de-seeded cucumber, 1 diced and de-seeded tomato, 1 teaspoon cumin seed, and 1 small handful of chopped mint, and season. Serve with naan bread.

Crab and cream cheese dip on prawn crackers

Spicy peanut dip

In a small bowl, use a fork to blend together 6 tablespoons chunky peanut butter, 3 tablespoons hoisin sauce, 1 teaspoon chilli sauce and 4 tablespoons water. Transfer the mixture to a serving bowl and provide sugar snap peas as crudités.

White bean dip

Drain a 400g (14oz) tin of cannellini beans and put the beans in a food processor. Add 1 anchovy, 1 garlic clove, juice of ½ lemon, and 2 tablespoons extra virgin olive oil, then season. Serve with crudités or fresh bread.

Salad is no longer just about leaves. Noodles, grains, and earthy vegetables have now moved into the this sphere. To create the dressing, seek out quality vinegars, oils, herbs, and spices. Zesty and downright delicious, these salads bring the promise of flavour and freshness.

Salads

Chunky chopped salad
with a red wine and caper vinaigrette

Recipes for chopped salads are easily transformed; substitute any ingredient for your favourite foods. Well-drained marinated artichoke hearts can be used in place of palm hearts, if you are unable to locate them.

1 Place all of the salad ingredients in a medium-sized bowl.

2 Add all of the vinaigrette ingredients to a small, lidded jar. Close the lid, shake well to combine, then pour over the salad. Mix well and serve.

Prepare ahead

The salad can be assembled, without the onion and basil, on the morning of serving, covered, and refrigerated. The vinaigrette can be made the day before, but don't add it until just before serving.

INGREDIENTS

2 red peppers, cut into 2½cm (1in) squares

125g (4oz) fresh bocconcini mini mozzarella balls, or 2 large ones, torn into pieces

200g (7oz) canned palm hearts, cut into 1cm (½in) slices

2 organic eggs or 5 quail's eggs, hard-boiled, peeled and quartered

125g (4oz) Italian salami, such as pepperoni, sliced

3 celery heart stalks with leaves, chopped

1 small red onion, finely diced

1 small bunch of fresh basil leaves, torn

Vinaigrette

2 tbsp red wine vinegar, such as cabernet sauvignon or chianti

3 tbsp extra virgin olive oil

½ garlic clove, finely chopped

1 tsp capers, rinsed and chopped

½ tsp each salt and pepper

Preparation time 20 minutes
Makes 8 small cups or 4 starters

BUY AND ARRANGE	PARTNER WITH
Smoked salmon blinis (see p148) • chocolate mint ice cream sandwiches (see p215) • white bean dip (see p71)	Halloumi and sourdough spiedini (see p106) • courgette ribbon rolls (see p160) • chocolate crinkle cookies (see p204)

Glass noodle salad
with black pepper chicken

Instead of the cellophane noodles, you could try very fine rice noodles, if you like. They will be have a more opaque look, but will still taste terrific.

1 To make the marinade, grind together the garlic, coriander, chilli, and pepper in a food processor or with a mortar and pestle. Add the sesame oil, fish sauce, and honey. Place the chicken in a bowl, coat with the marinade and leave for at least 30 minutes.

2 Remove the chicken from the marinade and pan-fry without any fat, or cook under the grill or on a barbecue, until very crispy and blackened on the edges. Chop into pieces.

3 Soak the noodles in boiling water for 5 minutes, or until al dente. Drain, rinse in cold water, then pat dry with kitchen towel. Cut the noodles in half with scissors and place in a bowl with the onion and herbs.

4 For the dressing, pound the garlic, chillis, sugar and ginger into a paste with a mortar and pestle. Stir in the lime juice and fish sauce. Pour over the salad and mix well. Arrange on bowls, top with the chicken, and sprinkle with any leftover herbs and peanuts.

Prepare ahead

The chicken may be left to marinate overnight in the refrigerator. The salad can be made 2 hours before serving, but add the herbs just before serving so that they keep their green colour.

BUY AND ARRANGE	PARTNER WITH
Asian cucumber salad (see p93) • selection of sushi (see p31) • fresh unpeeled lychees (see p215)	Seafood spring rolls (see p176) • five spice hoisin ribs (see p132) • miso halibut bites (see p140)

INGREDIENTS

1 garlic clove, peeled

Small handful coriander stems, finely chopped

1 tsp crushed dried chilli or fresh red chilli

1 tbsp freshly ground black pepper

2 tbsp sesame oil

2 tbsp fish sauce

1 tbsp honey

6 boneless, skinless chicken thighs (about 500g/1lb)

150g (5oz) cellophane noodles (mung beans or glass noodles)

1 red onion, finely sliced in half-moons

Large mixed handful of fresh mint, coriander, and basil (Thai if possible)

Crushed roasted peanuts, to garnish

Dressing

1 garlic clove, minced

½ medium red chilli, seeded and finely chopped

2 tbsp palm or soft brown sugar

1 tbsp grated ginger

Juice of 3 limes

2 tbsp fish sauce

Preparation and cooking time
30 minutes, plus 30 minutes marinating time

Makes 8 small salads

Farro salad
with anchovy, mint, and pecorino

Farro is a chewy-textured wheat grain that is often called spelt. Risotto rice can be used in its place but be sure to rinse well and cook al dente.

1 Preheat the oven to 180°C (350°F/Gas mark 4). Drain the farro, put it in a saucepan of salted water, and boil for 30 minutes, or until tender but not mushy. Meanwhile, place the tomatoes on a non-stick baking tray, drizzle with the oil, and season. Bake for 20 minutes, then remove from the oven, and leave to cool.

2 Place the onion in a large mixing bowl with the lemon juice and leave for 10 minutes to soften the flavour.

3 To make the dressing, heat the oil in a sauté pan, add the anchovy and garlic, and lightly brown. As soon as the garlic has coloured, add the vinegar, honey, salt, and pepper. Stir well until incorporated. Remove from the heat.

4 Drain the farro and stir it into the diced onion. Add the celery, pecorino, sultanas, and roasted tomatoes. Pour into the dressing, mix well, and stir in the herbs. Serve in individual bowls.

Prepare ahead

The dressed salad will keep for 2 hours, but may need a little extra olive oil or vinegar if it dries out. To retain their green colour, the herbs should be added just before serving.

INGREDIENTS

250g (8oz) farro, soaked for 1 hour in cold water

250g (8oz) baby plum or cherry tomatoes, halved

2 tbsp olive oil

½ tsp each salt and pepper

1 red onion, finely diced

Juice of ½ lemon

3 stalks of celery heart, finely sliced

60g (2oz) pecorino cheese, coarsely grated

4 tbsp sultanas, soaked in warm water for 10 minutes

Small handful each mint, basil, parsley, roughly chopped

Dressing

6 tbsp extra virgin olive oil

1 anchovy, rinsed and chopped

1 garlic clove, finely chopped

4 tbsp red wine vinegar

1 tsp honey

½ tsp each salt and pepper

Preparation time 30 minutes
Cooking time 30 minutes
Makes 8 small cups of salad or 4 starters

BUY AND ARRANGE	PARTNER WITH
Marinated anchovies (see p30) • marinated olives (see p30) • lemon curd spread on toasted brioche (see p214)	Fried artichokes Roman style (see p12) • mushroom and chestnut soup (see p38) • smoky aubergine purée (see p64)

Grilled aubergine salad
with pomegranate dressing

Pomegranate molasses is the concentrated juice of the seeds. Use one teaspoon of lemon juice or red wine vinegar mixed with one teaspoon of honey in its place, if you wish.

1 Preheat the grill to high. Place the peppers skin-side up on a non-stick baking sheet. Place under the grill, cook until blackened, then transfer to a plastic bag, seal, and allow to steam for 5 minutes. When cool enough, peel off the skins and discard, and set the flesh aside.

2 Brush the aubergines with the oil, sprinkle with the cinnamon, and season. Cook under the grill until crispy on both sides.

3 To make the dressing, place all of the ingredients in a lidded jar, close it, and shake to combine thoroughly.

4 Arrange the aubergine and pepper on individual plates. Scatter with the onion and feta, and sprinkle with the cumin seeds. Spoon over the dressing, garnish with the mint, and serve immediately.

Prepare ahead

The salad and dressing can be made on the morning of serving, but add the feta and onions just before serving. The onions can be chopped and soaked in lemon juice 2 hours ahead.

INGREDIENTS

2 red peppers, quartered

3–4 small aubergines, sliced lengthways into 2.5cm (1in) strips

6 tbsp extra virgin olive oil

½ tsp ground cinnamon

1 small red onion, sliced into half moons

200g (7oz) feta cheese, drained and cut into 1cm (½in) slices

1 tsp cumin seeds, toasted in a dry pan

Small bunch of mint leaves, roughly chopped, to garnish

Dressing

1 small garlic clove, crushed

Juice of 1 lemon

2 tsp pomegranate molasses

75ml (3fl oz) extra virgin olive oil

1 tsp each salt and pepper

Preparation time 30 minutes
Cooking time 15 minutes
Makes 8 small salads or 4 starters

BUY AND ARRANGE	PARTNER WITH
Yoghurt and dill dip (*see p71*) • spice-dusted prawns (*see p148*) • oranges with rose water (*see p214*)	Cumin lamb skewers (*see p112*) • saffron feta filo triangles (*see p182*) • cardamom-poached apricots (*see p211*)

Pan-fried halloumi salad
with olive and lemon dressing

Halloumi is a Cypriot cheese that takes on a golden colour and soft texture when pan-fried. The lemon olive dressing cuts sharply through the salty flavour of the cheese.

1 Put all of the dressing ingredients in a small bowl, mix together, and set aside. Cut off the peel from the oranges, removing the white pith at the same time. Separate the segments by cutting between the inner membranes with a small serrated knife.

2 Cut the halloumi into 16 pieces approximately 1cm (½in) thick and 3cm (1¼in) by 3cm (1¼in) square. Dust them with the flour and season. Heat the olive oil in a frying pan, until very hot. Add the halloumi to the pan in stages, and fry until coloured and crispy on both sides. Add more oil if the pan becomes too dry.

3 Arrange small stacks of halloumi and orange, then drizzle over the sauce and sprinkle with the parsley. Alternatively, scatter the halloumi and orange on a serving dish with the sauce and parsley.

Prepare ahead

The dressing can be made the day before. The oranges can be segmented and refrigerated on the morning of serving. The halloumi can be pan-fried 1 hour before serving, then reheated or served at room temperature.

INGREDIENTS

2 blood or navel oranges

500g (16oz) halloumi, drained

125g (4oz) flour

Salt and pepper

4 tbsp olive oil

Small bunch flat-leaf parsley, chopped

Dressing

3 tbsp virgin olive oil

10 mild black olives, pitted and finely chopped

Medium bunch flat-leaf parsley, finely chopped

1 tsp capers, rinsed and chopped

½ preserved lemon, rind only, rinsed and finely chopped

2 tsp red wine vinegar

1 small red onion, finely diced

Preparation time 30 minutes

Makes 8 small salads or
16 large starters

BUY AND ARRANGE

Pan-fried chorizo (*see p149*)
• roasted new potatoes with paprika (*see p173*) • marinated anchovies (*see p30*)

PARTNER WITH

Yellow lentil soup (*see p44*)
• romesco dip (*see p56*) •
Serrano-wrapped prawns
(*see p108*)

Spinach and peppered pear salad
with raspberry walnut oil dressing

Walnut oil can make even the most humble lettuce taste impressive. Buy it in small quantities, since it loses its nutty perfume after a short time.

1 Preheat the oven to 200°C (400°F/Gas mark 6). Spread the bread cubes out on a non-stick baking tray. Drizzle with the oil, and season. Bake for 6 minutes, until golden. Remove the croûtons from the oven and leave to cool.

2 Roughly chop the pears into 1cm (½in) wide slices. Transfer to a small bowl with the freshly ground pepper and 1 tablespoon of the lemon juice, then toss to coat. In another bowl, mix together the onion and remaining juice.

3 Pour the dressing ingredients into a jar, close the lid, and shake well to combine. Arrange the spinach, pears, pecans, Parmesan crisps, and croûtons in small individual bowls. Just before serving, pour over the dressing.

Prepare ahead

The Parmesan crisps, toasted nuts, croûtons, and dressing can all be made the day before, and stored in separate airtight containers. The onion can be chopped and marinated in the lemon juice on the morning of serving.

INGREDIENTS

2.5cm (1in) cubes sourdough or French stick, about 2 large handfuls

3 tbsp olive oil

2 ripe comice or similar pears, quartered and cored

1 tbsp freshly ground pink and black peppercorns

Juice of 2 lemons

1 small red onion, finely diced

8 large handfuls of baby spinach or mesclun (mixed baby lettuces)

100g (3½oz) pecans, toasted

1 recipe Parmesan crisps (*see p31*) or 45g (1½oz) thickly grated Parmesan

Dressing

2 tbsp balsamic vinegar

1 tbsp raspberry vinegar

1 tbsp Dijon mustard

½ garlic clove, finely chopped

1 shallot, finely chopped

5 tbsp walnut or hazelnut oil

½ tsp each salt and pepper

Preparation time 20 minutes
Cooking time 6 minutes
Makes 8–10 individual cups or 4–6 starters

BUY AND ARRANGE	PARTNER WITH
Grilled asparagus with balsamic vinegar (*see p172*) • crushed feta dip (*see p70*) • prosciutto-wrapped melon (*see p31*)	Mozzarella en corrozza (*see p22*) • prawns and roasted tomatoes (*see p145*) • chocolate crinkle cookies (*see p204*)

Three tomato salad
with goat's cheese and croûtons

The types of tomatoes listed here are just a guide. Choose a selection of beautiful, ripe varieties. Using both red and yellow tomatoes adds colour and interest.

1 Preheat the oven to 200°C (400°F/Gas mark 6). On a baking sheet, toss the bread cubes with the oil, salt, and pepper. Bake for 6 minutes until light and golden. Avoid overcooking: you want chewy, not rock-hard, centres. Remove from the oven and leave to cool. Meanwhile toss the shallots with the lemon juice in a bowl.

2 Place all of the dressing ingredients in a jar, close the lid, and shake well to combine. In a large bowl, combine the tomatoes and basil. Pour over the dressing and turn to coat. Divide the salad between 6–8 small bowls, sprinkle with the goat's cheese, and serve.

Prepare ahead

The croûtons can be made 2 days in advance and stored in an airtight container. The dressing can be prepared the day before. The tomatoes can be cut 2 hours in advance, but drain off any excess juice before mixing the salad.

INGREDIENTS

520g (18oz) sourdough, French stick, or ciabatta bread, cut into 1cm (½in) cubes

2 tbsp extra virgin olive oil

½ tsp each salt and pepper

2 large shallots, finely diced

Juice of ½ lemon

500g (1lb) ripe cherry, teardrop, plum, or grape tomatoes, halved

2 zebra-striped or yellow tomatoes, quartered

2 yellow and/or red beefsteak or marmande tomatoes, cut into bite-sized chunks

Large bunch of basil, roughly chopped

100g (3½oz) firm, mild goat's cheese such as chèvre blanc, crumbled

Dressing

½ garlic clove, chopped

1½ tbsp red wine vinegar such as cabernet sauvignon

3½ tbsp extra virgin olive oil

½ tsp Dijon mustard

Pinch each of salt, pepper, and sugar

Preparation time 10 minutes
Cooking time 6 minutes
Makes 6–8 small salads

BUY AND ARRANGE	PARTNER WITH
Carrots in vinaigrette (see p173) • proscuitto-wrapped melon (see p31) • fresh crab crostini (see p148)	Sicilian artichoke bottoms (see p154) • bresaola and pear rolls (see p188) • chocolate Frangelico pudding (see p200)

Arabian salad
with dill and crispy pitta

This lively and colourful salad is a superb addition to any Middle Eastern or Moorish-inspired menu. The punchy flavours can liven up an otherwise plain meat or fish dish.

1 Preheat the oven to 200°C (400°F/Gas mark 6). Place the diced pitta bread on a non-stick baking sheet, spoon over the olive oil, and turn to coat. Bake for about 5 minutes, turning once, until golden and crisp. Remove and leave to cool.

2 To make the dressing, put all the ingredients in a small glass jar, close the lid, and shake well until thoroughly mixed.

3 In a large bowl, combine the lettuce, tomatoes, cucumber, spring onions, red pepper, radishes, herbs, and pitta crisps.

4 Pour the dressing over the salad, season to taste, and toss well. Divide between 8 small bowls or 4 starter plates. Sprinkle with the pomegranate seeds, if using.

Prepare ahead

The pitta crisps can be baked and stored in an airtight container for 4 days. The dressing can be made the night before. The salad ingredients can be prepared about 4 hours in advance and kept covered in the refrigerator until ready to combine.

INGREDIENTS

6 pitta breads, cut into tiny squares with scissors

3 tbsp extra virgin olive oil

1 small head romaine or 2 baby gem lettuce, cut into small pieces

250g (9oz) cherry tomatoes, halved

1 medium-sized cucumber, de-seeded, or 3 Lebanese mini cucumbers, diced

4 spring onions, thinly sliced

1 red pepper, diced

6 radishes, thinly sliced

1 small bunch of fresh dill, chopped

1 small bunch fresh mint, finely chopped

Pomegranate seeds, to garnish

Dressing

1 small garlic clove, crushed

½ tsp each salt and pepper

1 tsp lemon juice

2 tsp red wine vinegar or pomegranate molasses

75ml (3fl oz) extra virgin olive oil

Preparation time 20 minutes
Makes 8 small bowls or 4 starters

BUY AND ARRANGE	PARTNER WITH
Houmous with smoked paprika (*see p70*) • pan-fried chorizo (*see p149*) • Middle Eastern pastries (*see p214*)	Spinach and yoghurt dip (*see p66*) • saffron feta filo triangles (*see p182*) • cumin lamb skewers (*see p112*)

Seared duck and mango salad
with green papaya

Green papaya can be found in Thai supermarkets. To preserve its crunch, don't grate it but slice into julienne. If you can't find green papaya, substitute with rice noodles.

1 Preheat the oven to 200°C (400°F/Gas mark 6). Using a sharp knife, cut a cross-hatch pattern into the duck skin. Combine the the marinade ingredients and place in a bowl. Add the duck breasts, coat, and leave to marinate for at least 15 minutes.

2 Heat a non-stick pan until very hot. Meanwhile, remove the duck from the marinade, wipe, place skin-side down in the pan, and brown. Reduce the heat to low and continue to cook until the fat is melted and the skin is thin and crispy. Place the duck on a non-stick baking tray and bake in the oven for 10 minutes. Remove and allow to rest for 10 minutes before slicing thinly.

3 Divide the papaya, mango, and herbs between 8 small bowls. Top with the duck, garnish with spring onion, and pour over the lime chilli dressing. Sprinkle with the peanuts and serve.

Prepare ahead

The duck can be left to marinate overnight in the refrigerator. The salad ingredients and dressing can be assembled on the morning of serving, and tossed just before serving. The salad can be dressed 1 hour before serving.

INGREDIENTS

2 duck breasts

1 medium green papaya, sliced into julienne strips

1 very firm mango, sliced into julienne strips

Small handful Thai or Mediterranean basil leaves

Small handful mint leaves

Small handful coriander leaves

4 spring onions, shredded lengthways

1 recipe lime chilli dressing (*see p216*), to serve

3 tbsp crushed roasted peanuts, to garnish

Marinade

2 tbsp soy sauce

1 tbsp honey

1 tbsp grated ginger

1 tsp cracked black pepper

Preparation and cooking time
35 minutes, plus 15 minutes marinating time

Makes 8 small salads or 4 starters

BUY AND ARRANGE	PARTNER WITH
Fresh oysters on the shell (*see p148*) • selection of sushi (*see p31*) • freshly sliced pineapple (*see p215*)	Pork and prawn dumplings (*see p184*) • crispy scallops (*see p24*) • miso monkfish bites (*see p140*)

Quick salads
buy and arrange ideas to create simple salads

With just a few raw ingredients, some washing, a little chopping, and a quickly mixed dressing, you can create a myriad of enticing, fresh salads. Try any of the ideas below as a quick alternative to the other salad dishes featured in this chapter. These short recipes are just a guide, so experiment with different leaves and dressings.

Shaved celery salad with mushroom and pecorino

Slice enough white mushrooms and celery hearts to make 2 handfuls of each. Mix them in a bowl with 1 handful grated pecorino. In a separate bowl, mix 1 tablespoon red wine vinegar with 2 tablespoons extra virgin olive oil, then season. Serve the salad drizzled with the dressing.

Fig, prosciutto, and mozzarella salad

Cut 4 ripe figs and 4 slices of prosciutto into quarters and arrange them on a platter with a small bunch of basil leaves. Rip 2 mozzarella balls into small pieces and add them to the plate. Drizzle over the platter with 1 tablespoon balsamic vinegar and 2 tablespoons extra virgin olive oil, then season. Serve the salad on the platter or in separate small bowls.

Baby lettuce with walnut oil and sherry vinegar

Place 5 generous handfuls of fresh mixed baby lettuces in a mixing bowl. In a separate bowl, mix 1 tablespoon sherry vinegar with 2 tablespoons walnut oil, then season. Toss the salad with the dressing then divide between small serving bowls.

Palm heart and avocado salad

Drain a 400g (14oz) tin of palm hearts. Slice the palm hearts and 2 avocados into chunky pieces and place them in a bowl. Add a small handful of thickly grated parmesan and combine well. In a separate bowl, mix 1 tablespoon red wine vinegar and 2 tablespoons extra virgin olive oil, then season. Serve the salad in small bowls, drizzled with the dressing.

Radicchio, orange, and rocket salad

Mix together 2 large handfuls of both rocket and chopped radicchio leaves in a bowl. Cut the segments from 2 oranges and add to the salad. In a separate bowl, mix 1 tablespoon balsamic vinegar and 2 tablespoons extra virgin olive oil then season. Toss the salad with the dressing and serve in small bowls.

Tomato and coconut sambal

In a bowl, mix together 2 large handfuls of chopped cherry tomatoes; 1 medium cucumber, diced; 1 small red onion, diced; 1 small handful chopped coriander; 2 tablespoons shredded coconut, ½ teaspoon cumin seeds; ½ teaspoon chilli powder, and the juice of ½ a lemon. Serve in small bowls.

Watermelon and feta salad

Cut a small watermelon into cubes or slices and arrange on a platter, or on smaller serving plates. Add 1 small handful of mint leaves, a chunk of feta, crumbled, and 1 thinly sliced red onion. In a separate bowl, mix the juice of 1 lemon, 1 tablespoon balsamic vinegar and 1 tablespoon extra virgin olive oil, then drizzle over the salad.

Frisée with quail's eggs

In a bowl, mix 1 tablespoon red wine vinegar with 2 tablespoons extra virgin olive oil, then season. Mix the dressing with 5 handfuls of frisée lettuce and transfer to small serving bowls. Top with 6 halved soft-boiled quail's eggs.

Chicory salad with anchovy lemon dressing

Using a pestle and mortar, pound together 1 anchovy and 1 garlic clove. Mix in the juice of 1 lemon and 2 tablespoons extra virgin olive oil. Mix the dressing with 4 heads of chicory in a bowl and season. Serve in small bowls.

Watercress salad with spring onion

In a bowl, toss together 5 large handfuls of watercress or other spicy lettuce with 2 sliced spring onions. In a separate bowl, mix together 1 tablespoon sesame seeds, 1 teaspoon soy sauce, 1 teaspoon balsamic vinegar, and 1 tablespoon olive oil, then season. Toss the salad with the dressing and serve in small bowls.

Watermelon and feta salad

Asian cucumber salad

Thinly slice 4 tiny cucumbers or cut 1 large cucumber into 2cm (¾in) cubes. In a small bowl, mix together 1 tablespoon rice wine vinegar, with 1 teaspoon sugar, then season. Mix the cucumber cubes or slices with the dressing, then serve in small bowls.

Lebanese salad plate

Arrange the leaves of 1 small romaine heart, some halved Lebanese cucumbers, or very small cucumbers, a handful of whole radishes, sprigs of fresh parsley and tarragon, and 1 thickly sliced red pepper on a serving plate.

What is it about food on a stick that makes it so enticing? Perhaps it is the ease of sliding off each bite as you eat, savouring the taste, then casually discarding the skewer. Choose your sticks with flair; metal or bamboo skewers are fine, but lemongrass stalks or sugar cane are more interesting.

Skewers

Citrus swordfish brochettes
with pomegranate dipping sauce

Swordfish is a meaty, firm type of fish, which makes it particularly well-suited for threading onto skewers. The sharp, citrus flavours complement its subtle flavour.

1 Rub the fish with the olive oil and garlic, then sprinkle with the lemon and orange zest, chillies, fennel seed, salt, and pepper. Leave to marinate in the refrigerator for 30 minutes to 2 hours.

2 Thread two pieces of fish onto each skewer. Place in a non-stick frying pan and dry-fry until browned on all sides. This cooking method creates the best colour but you could also cook the skewers under the grill or on a barbecue. Serve with the pomegranate dipping sauce and lemon or lime wedges.

Prepare ahead

The dipping sauce, fish cubes, and marinade ingredients may be prepared the day before and refrigerated. You can pan-fry the fish 2 hours before serving, but leave it underdone and gently reheat in an oven preheated to 200°C (400°F/Gas mark 6).

INGREDIENTS

500g (1lb) swordfish, cut into 50 x 2.5cm (1in) cubes

1 tbsp extra virgin olive oil

1 garlic clove, crushed

Zest of 1 lemon, grated

Zest of 1 orange, grated

½ tsp crushed dried chillies

1½ tbsp fennel seed, crushed in a mortar and pestle

½ tsp each salt and pepper

25 metal or wooden skewers (if wooden, soak in water for 1 hour to prevent burning)

1 recipe pomegranate dipping sauce (see p216), to serve

Lemon or lime wedges, to serve

Preparation and cooking time
20 minutes
Makes 25 skewers

BUY AND ARRANGE

Houmous with smoked paprika (see p70) • watermelon and feta salad (see p93) • Middle Eastern pastries (see p214)

PARTNER WITH

Yellow lentil soup (see p44) • chickpea and chilli dip (see p68) • pan-fried halloumi salad (see p82)

Saffron chicken skewers
with sweet tomato jam

This marinade is based on the Spanish tapas dish pinchitos murunos, consisting of pork fillet grilled with saffron and spices. Pimenton (sweet, smoked Spanish paprika) may be found in good delicatessens or larger supermarkets.

1 Combine all of the marinade ingredients in a bowl, mixing thoroughly. Flatten the cubes of chicken slightly, add to the marinade, and turn to coat on all sides. Leave to marinate in the refrigerator for at least 1–2 hours.

2 Preheat the oven to 200°C (400°F/Gas mark 6). Thread one piece of chicken onto each skewer and season. Heat the oil in a non-stick frying pan, add the skewers, and fry to colour each side. Transfer to a non-stick baking sheet, cover with foil, and place in the oven for 5 minutes. Alternatively, cook the skewers under the grill or on a barbecue.

3 Arrange the chicken skewers on a serving plate, garnish with the coriander and serve with the sweet tomato jam.

Prepare ahead
The jam can be prepared up to 4 days in advance. The skewers may be marinated 1 day ahead and pan-fried up to 2 hours before cooking in the oven.

INGREDIENTS

3 chicken breasts or boneless skinless thighs, cut into 25 x 2.5cm (1in) cubes

25 wooden skewers, soaked in water for 1 hour, to prevent burning

Salt and pepper

1–2 tbsp olive oil

1 recipe sweet tomato jam (*see p218*), to serve

A few sprigs coriander, to garnish

Marinade

½ tsp each coriander seeds, cumin seeds, and fennel seeds, roughly ground

1 tsp pimenton

2 garlic cloves, crushed

Pinch of saffron, infused in 1 tbsp boiling water

1 tbsp red wine vinegar

1 tbsp olive oil

Preparation time 10 minutes
Cooking time 15 minutes
Makes 25 skewers

BUY AND ARRANGE	PARTNER WITH
Roasted new potatoes with paprika (*see p173*) • crushed feta dip (*see p70*) • spice-dusted prawns (*see p148*)	Pan-fried haloumi salad (*see p82*) • smoky aubergine purée (*see p64*) • Arabian salad (*see p88*)

Colours

- Creamy ivory
- Warm tangerine
- Rose pink
- Gold or silver
- Cool violet

Tableware

- Tea lights and candles
- Gold-rimmed glasses
- Creamy-coloured linens
- Red rose petals
- Embroidered napkins

Middle Eastern delights

Pack your bags for the spice trail. The journey begins in Iran, then continues on through Turkey, stays a little while in Morrocco, and lingers in Spain. These countries' cuisines have each been moulded by the Arabs, who left behind a legacy of Persian cooking brilliance.

A traditional Middle Eastern meal is made up of a variety of smaller dishes, and this is the classic style of mezze and tapas. These diminutive little bites, from chickpea dips to savoury pastries, offer your taste buds truly memorable eating experiences. Lemons, olives, coriander, saffron, rose water, dried apricots, and pistachios are the stars of this exemplary food. Aromatic spices, fresh herbs, flaky pastry, and creamy pulses are present in endless, delicious variations.

So, light every candle you own and fill your home with a sensual glow. For the table, seek out creamy-coloured linens and lightweight fabrics, such as voile, gold-rimmed glassware and tea glasses, and scatter over red rose petals. Picture Arabian nights and re-create that soft, romantic atmosphere that makes the Middle East so special.

Flavours

- Pungent cumin
- Sharp lemon
- Luxurious saffron
- Dried fruits
- Fragrant rose water

Nibbles

- Pistachios (*see p31*)
- Marinated black olives (*see p30*)
- Houmous with smoked paprika (*see p70*)
- Sumac-dusted prawns (*see p148*)
- Crushed feta dip (*see p70*)

Menu

Chickpea and chilli dip
with pitta crisps

Saffron chicken skewers
with sweet tomato jam

Saffron feta filo triangles
with preserved lemon and onion

Pan-fried halloumi salad
with black olive dressing

Yellow lentil soup with prunes,
pomegranates, and apricots

Cardamom-poached apricots
with mascarpone and pistachios

BUY AND ARRANGE
Marinated black olives (*see p30*)

Oranges with rose water and
pomegranate seeds (*see p214*)

Crushed feta dip (*see p70*)

Chickpea and chilli dip
(*see p68*)

Saffron chicken skewers
(*see p98*)

Saffron feta filo triangles
(*see p182*)

Pan-fried halloumi salad
(*see p82*)

Yellow lentil soup
(*see p44*)

Cardamom-poached
apricots (*see p211*)

Two days before
- Make sweet tomato jam
- Make yellow lentil soup
- Marinate black olives

The night before
- Make pitta crisps for the
  chickpea dip
- Marinate saffron chicken
- Assemble saffron feta filo
  triangles
- Make cardamom-poached
  apricots

In the morning
- Purée base of chickpea dip
- Cut oranges and make black
  olive dressing for halloumi salad
- Make oranges with rose water

Orange champagne cocktails

Oranges are a quintessential fruit of the Middle East and they act as the perfect partner to champagne.

INGREDIENTS

6 measures of orange vodka

6 sugar cubes

6 raspberries

6 dashes of angostura bitter

1 bottle champagne or sparkling white wine

Zest of 1 orange

Makes 6 cocktails

Add 1 measure of vodka, 1 sugar cube, 1 raspberry, and 1 dash of angostura bitter to each champagne glass. Pour the champagne over. Use cubes of orange or pomegranate seeds in place of the raspberries, if you wish. Serve topped with small slivers of orange zest.

One to two hours before
- Finish chickpea dip
- Sear saffron chicken
- Pan-fry halloumi for the salad
- Plate cardamom-poached apricots
- Reheat yellow lentil soup
- Organise cocktail ingredients

Half an hour before
- Reheat sweet tomato jam
- Cook saffron chicken skewers
- Plate oranges with rose water
- Bake saffron feta filo triangles

Half an hour before
- Plate chickpea dip with pitta crisps
- Plate saffron chicken skewers
- Plate halloumi salad with black olive dressing
- Plate saffron feta filo triangles
- Pour yellow lentil soup
- Pour champagne cocktails

Lemongrass beef skewers
with sticky cucumber and peanut sauce

If you are short on time, serve these skewers with a bottled sweet chilli dipping sauce. Sirloin or rump steak, cut into very thin strips, can be used in place of the beef fillet.

1 If using beef fillet, cut into 4cm (1½in) cubes. If using sirloin or rump steak, cut into very thin strips. Cut away the top two thirds of the lemongrass stalks, remove the outer leaves, and chop the hearts finely.

2 Combine the lemongrass, garlic, fish sauce, sesame oil, five spice powder, honey, and coriander in a shallow bowl. Add the beef, turn to coat, and marinate for at least 10 minutes. Remove the meat from the marinade and thread the beef onto the skewers.

3 Heat the vegetable oil in a non-stick frying pan. Add the skewers and brown on all sides: they will need only a few minutes since the meat is very tender. Remove from the heat, cover with foil, and leave to rest for 5 minutes. Alternatively, cook under the grill or on a barbecue. Serve the skewers on lettuce leaves, accompanied by the sticky cucumber and peanut sauce.

Prepare ahead

The meat can be marinated up to 2 days ahead and the sauce can be made on the morning of serving. Grill and par-cook the skewers a few hours ahead, refrigerate, then complete cooking just before serving.

INGREDIENTS

500g (1lb) beef fillet, sirloin, or rump steak

4 lemongrass stalks

2 garlic cloves, finely chopped

2 tbsp fish sauce

2 tbsp sesame oil

1½ tsp five spice powder

2 tbsp honey

1 small bunch coriander, chopped

25 metal or wooden skewers (if wooden, soak for 30 minutes to prevent burning)

1 tbsp vegetable oil

Lettuce leaves, to serve

1 recipe sticky cucumber and peanut sauce (see p218), to serve

Preparation and cooking time
30 minutes
Makes 20–25 skewers

BUY AND ARRANGE

Asian cucumber salad (*see p93*) • spicy peanut dip (*see p71*) • exotic fruit salad (*see p215*)

PARTNER WITH

Seared sesame tuna (*see p138*) • pork satay (*see p109*) • avocado crostini (*see p164*)

Halloumi and sourdough spiedini
with lemon anchovy drizzle

Mozzarella is great in place of the halloumi here, but it melts quickly, so keep a careful eye on it. Use a different bread, if you prefer, but remember to have a little crust on each cube so that they stay on the skewer.

1 Cut the halloumi into 32x 2½cm (1in) cubes. Slice the bread into 32 x 2½cm (1in) cubes, retaining the crusts for strength.

2 To make the drizzle, crush the garlic and anchovies to a paste with a mortar and pestle. Transfer to a saucepan. Add the butter and olive oil and simmer over a low heat for 5 minutes. Remove from the heat and stir in the lemon juice, zest, and parsley.

3 Thread the cheese and bread onto the skewers, alternating 2 cubes of bread and 2 pieces of cheese. Brush with the drizzle and season. Pan-fry in a non-stick frying pan until golden on all sides. Alternatively, cook under the grill or on a barbecue.

Prepare ahead
The ingredients can be prepared on the morning of serving, stored in the refrigerator, then brushed with the drizzle just before cooking.

INGREDIENTS

800g (28oz) halloumi

Small loaf of sourdough bread

16 x 15cm (6in) wooden skewers, pre-soaked to prevent burning

Drizzle

1 garlic clove, finely chopped

2 anchovies, rinsed and finely chopped

30g (1oz) unsalted butter

4 tbsp extra virgin olive oil

Juice of 1½ lemons

1 tsp lemon zest

Small handful fresh parsley, finely chopped

Preparation time 20 minutes
Cooking time 15 minutes
Makes 16 skewers

BUY AND ARRANGE

Shaved celery salad (*see p92*) • avocado with balsamic vinegar (*see p173*) • radishes with tapenade (*see p173*)

PARTNER WITH

Meatball and pecorino soup (*see p48*) • roasted prawns and tomatoes (*see p145*) • chocolate Frangelico pudding (*see p200*)

Serrano-wrapped prawns
with roasted pepper salsa

Piquillo peppers are a smoked, roasted Spanish pepper sold in jars and located in many supermarkets. If you can't find them, use two large roasted red peppers instead.

1 Wrap each prawn in a strip of ham, then thread onto a skewer.

2 To make the salsa, heat 4 tablespoons of the oil in a saucepan. Add the garlic slices and sauté on a low heat for 3–5 minutes, until golden brown. Remove the garlic and set aside.

3 Add the vinegar, honey, salt, and pepper to the oil in the pan, and whisk over a low heat, until combined. Transfer to a small bowl and stir in the garlic, onion, pepper, and parsley.

4 To make the skewers, heat the oil in a frying pan until hot, and fry the skewers for about 1 minute on all sides, until the ham is golden and the prawns are cooked through. Arrange the salsa in small bowls and top each with 1–2 skewers.

Prepare ahead

The skewers and salsa can be assembled the day before, and refrigerated. Bring the salsa to room temperature before serving.

INGREDIENTS

24 large prawns, peeled and de-veined

8 slices Serrano ham or prosciutto, cut into 3 strips

24 wooden skewers, soaked in water for 30 minutes

1 tbsp extra virgin olive oil

Salsa

4 tbsp extra virgin olive oil

2 garlic cloves, thinly sliced

2 tbsp sherry vinegar

2 tsp honey

½ tsp each salt and pepper

1 small red onion, finely diced

8 piquillo peppers, finely diced

4 tbsp finely chopped, fresh flat-leaf parsley

Preparation time 30 minutes
Cooking time 10 minutes
Makes 24 skewers

BUY AND ARRANGE

Palm heart and avocado salad (see p92) • crushed feta dip (see p70) • ice cream with sweet sherry (see p214)

PARTNER WITH

Crispy chorizo quesadillas (see p186) • beef and sweet potato skewers (see p114) • beetroot pesto (see p67)

Pork satay on lemongrass
with spicy peanut sauce

The lemongrass skewers add fragrance and interest, but use pre-soaked wooden skewers instead if you wish.

1 Preheat the oven to 200°C (400°F/Gas mark 6). Trim the tops of 4 lemongrass stalks, remove leaves, and chop hearts finely. In a bowl, mix the coriander, chopped lemongrass, pork, garlic, shallots, fish sauce, cornflour, curry paste, and pepper. Shape into 20 balls.

2 Slice the remaining lemongrass lengthways to make 20 sticks. With flour-dusted hands, thread the meatballs onto the skewers, moulding them on. Sprinkle with the castor sugar and set aside.

3 Heat the oil in a frying pan and fry the skewers for 1 minute on each side, until golden. Place on a non-stick baking tray, cover with foil, and bake in the oven for 5 minutes. Garnish with coriander and serve with the spicy peanut sauce.

Prepare ahead

Prepare the sauce and meatballs a day ahead and refrigerate. The meat can be threaded onto the skewers on the morning of serving.

INGREDIENTS

16 lemongrass stalks

Small bunch fresh coriander, chopped, a few sprigs saved to garnish

500g (1lb) lean minced pork

3 garlic cloves, finely chopped

3 shallots, finely chopped

2 tbsp fish sauce

1 egg, beaten

1 tbsp red curry paste

½ tsp pepper

2 tbsp rice or plain flour, for dusting

1 tbsp vegetable oil

1 recipe spicy peanut sauce (*see p218*), to serve

Preparation time 20 minutes
Cooking time 30 minutes
Makes 20 skewers

BUY AND ARRANGE

Caramelized grilled pineapple (*see p214*) • prawn and cucumber skewers (*see p149*) • steamed edamame (*see p173*)

PARTNER WITH

Thai sweetcorn fritters (*see p26*) • red curry pumpkin soup (*see p46*) • seared duck and mango salad (*see p90*)

Salmon pineapple skewers
with chilli glaze and lime crème fraîche

Dried chillies impart a depth to glazes and sauces that fresh chillies can't match. Anchos have a subtle, fruity scent. Use any other large dried variety if you can't find them.

1 To make the glaze, place the chilli in a bowl of boiling water and leave it to soak for 15 minutes. Meanwhile, in a large, dry, non-stick frying pan, pan-fry the garlic and onion over a medium low heat, stirring, for about 7 minutes, until blackened on all sides. Remove from the heat and allow to cool, then peel the garlic.

2 Drain the chilli and place it in a blender or food processor with the garlic, onion, vinegar, sugar, and salt. Purée until smooth, then pour into a small bowl. In a separate bowl, mix the lime zest and juice with the crème fraîche, and set aside.

3 Preheat the oven to 200°C (400°F/Gas mark 6). Thread one salmon and one pineapple cube onto each skewer. Brush with the glaze. Heat the oil in a non-stick frying pan, cook the skewers in batches, searing for 1 minute to colour each side. Place on a baking sheet, cover with foil, and heat through in the oven for 5 minutes. Alternatively, the skewers can be grilled or barbecued. Serve with coriander sprigs and the lime crème fraîche.

Prepare ahead

The glaze can be made 1 week in advance and refrigerated. The skewers can be assembled the day before and refrigerated.

INGREDIENTS

200g (7fl oz) crème fraîche or sour cream

Juice and grated zest of 1 lime

500g (1lb) thick salmon fillet, sliced into 2.5cm (1in) cubes

1 small pineapple, cut into 2.5cm (1in) cubes

20 metal or wooden skewers (if wooden, soak in water for 30 minutes to prevent burning)

2 tbsp vegetable oil

Chopped fresh coriander, to garnish

Glaze

1 dried ancho, de-seeded and stem removed

6 garlic cloves, unpeeled

1 small yellow onion, thickly sliced

60ml (2fl oz) cider vinegar

4 tbsp soft brown sugar

½ tsp salt

Preparation time 40 minutes
Cooking time 20 minutes
Makes 20–25 skewers

BUY AND ARRANGE	PARTNER WITH
Sweet potato wedges with cumin (see p172) • fruit salsa (see p70) • mango fool (see p215)	Smoky black bean dip (see p58) • grilled butterflied prawns (see p141) • crab and gruyére nachos (see p142)

Cumin lamb skewers
with red onion parsley salad

Use the soft flatbread to scoop up luscious mouthfuls of the salad and lamb. If you can't find the molasses, use a tablespoon each of honey and lemon juice in its place.

1 Combine the marinade ingredients in a medium-sized bowl. Add the lamb, toss to coat, and leave to marinate for at least 30 minutes. Thread one or two lamb cubes onto each skewer, then set aside until ready to grill.

2 For the salad, place the onions in a bowl with the lemon juice, salt, and pepper. Turn to coat and leave for 5 minutes to reduce the raw taste of the onion. Add the parsley, paprika, and oil. Mix well and set aside.

3 Heat the vegetable oil in a non-stick frying pan. Add the skewers and brown the meat well on all sides. Remove and place under foil for 5 minutes to rest. Alternatively, grill the skewers or cook over a barbecue. Serve on small plates or on a platter with the salad and pitta. Garnish with pomegranate seeds, if liked.

Prepare ahead

The lamb can be left to marinate up to 2 days in advance. It may then be browned 4 hours before serving, refrigerated, and finished off for 5 minutes in an oven heated to 200°C (400°F/Gas mark 6). The salad may be assembled 2 hours in advance.

INGREDIENTS

500g (1lb) lamb fillet, chump or leg steaks, cut into 4cm (1½in) cubes

20–25 skewers (if wooden, soak for 30 minutes to prevent burning)

1 tbsp vegetable oil

Pitta or other flatbread, to serve

Fresh pomegranate seeds, to garnish (*optional*)

Marinade

4 tbsp pomegranate molasses

1 tsp cumin seeds, lightly toasted

4 garlic cloves, crushed

1 tsp each salt and pepper

Salad

1 red onion, cut into thin half-moons

Juice of ½ lemon

½ tsp each salt and pepper

1 large handful of parsley leaves, roughly chopped

½ tsp paprika or sumac

1 tbsp extra virgin olive oil

Preparation and cooking time
20 minutes, plus 30 minutes to overnight marinating time

Makes 20–25 skewers

BUY AND ARRANGE	PARTNER WITH
Roasted new potatoes with paprika (*see p173*) • yoghurt and dill dip (*see p71*) • black olives with orange (*see p30*)	Spinach and yoghurt dip (*see p66*) • saffron feta filo triangles (*see p182*) • Arabian salad (*see p88*)

Beef and sweet potato skewers
with chimmichuri sauce

Chimmichuri is a punchy chilli and herb sauce from South America and it pairs well with meat. Other tender cuts of beef can work nearly as well as fillets.

1 Combine the marinade ingredients in a bowl, stirring well to mix. Add the meat, turn to coat, and leave to marinate for an hour.

2 Meanwhile, preheat the oven to 200°C (400°F/Gas mark 6). Place the sweet potato pieces in a roasting tin with the oil, turn to coat, season, and roast for 20 minutes. Remove from the oven and leave to cool.

3 To make the sauce, place all of the ingredients in a bowl and mix well. The chopping and mixing can be done in a food processor for a smoother consistency, adding the chillies and garlic first.

4 Thread the skewers with the meat and sweet potato. Set aside. Heat the grill to high and grill the skewers for about 2 minutes on each side, until crispy on the edges. Cover with foil and allow to rest for 5 minutes before serving warm, with the sauce. Alternatively, they can be cooked on a barbecue.

Prepare ahead

The beef can be marinated for up to 2 days, covered in the refrigerator, and skewered the day before serving. The sauce can be made 4 hours in advance.

INGREDIENTS

500g (1lb) beef fillet or sirloin steak, cut into 4cm (1½in) cubes

3 sweet potatoes, cut into 4cm (1½in) chunks

2 tbsp olive oil

20 metal or wooden skewers (if wooden, soak in water for 30 minutes to prevent burning)

Marinade

1 tbsp olive oil

1 tbsp ground cumin

½ tsp each salt and pepper

Sauce

1 jalapeño or other green chilli, de-seeded and finely chopped

2 garlic cloves, finely chopped

Small bunch fresh coriander, finely chopped

Large bunch flat-leaf parsley, finely chopped

½ tsp pimenton

125ml (4fl oz) extra virgin olive oil

3 tbsp red wine vinegar, such as cabernet sauvignon or strong Chianti

½ tsp each and pepper

Preparation time 20 minutes, plus 1 hour marinating time

Cooking time 25 minutes

Makes 20 skewers

BUY AND ARRANGE	PARTNER WITH
Palm heart and avocado salad (see p92) • Spanish deli plate (see p30) • pan-fried chorizo (see p149)	Smoky blackbean dip (see p58) • crab and gruyére nachos (see p142) • grilled butterflied prawns (see p141)

Whether you prefer to use the bones of cutlets as natural brochettes, or decide to choose a faithful fork, eating meat is a tactile experience with a primitive allure. Pair with some fresh herbs and spices or marinate in zesty sauces, and you are ready for some serious sustenance.

Meat

Rosemary lamb chops
with fresh mint and parsley sauce

This simple but exquisite dish works best using two racks of lamb. Buy them cleaned of fat so the chops can be picked up and eaten by hand. Alternatively, use 12 lamb cutlets.

1 Combine the oil, vinegar, and rosemary in a large bowl. Cover with a sheet of greaseproof paper or baking parchment and flatten slightly with a rolling pin or meat mallet. Add to the oil mixture, turn to coat, and leave to marinate for at least 1 hour.

2 Preheat the grill to very hot. Remove the chops from the marinade and cook under the grill for 2 minutes on each side. Cover with foil and leave to rest for a few minutes before serving with the fresh mint and parsley sauce.

Prepare ahead

The chops can be marinated, covered, and refrigerated up to 2 days in advance. The sauce may be made on the morning of serving.

INGREDIENTS

1 tbsp olive oil

2 tbsp balsamic vinegar

1 tbsp fresh chopped rosemary

2 racks of lamb, cut into chops and bones cleaned of fat

1 recipe fresh mint and parsley sauce (see p216), to serve

Preparation time 15 minutes, plus 1 hour marinating time

Cooking time 8 minutes

Makes 12 cutlets

BUY AND ARRANGE

Frisée with quail's eggs (see p93) • roasted shallots (see p173) • biscotti, mascarpone, and dessert wine (see p215)

PARTNER WITH

Fried artichokes Roman style (see p12) • orange and beetroot soup (see p40) • farro salad (see p78)

Crispy pork larb and mango
in lettuce cups with chilli lime dressing

Larb means "chopped meat" in Thai. In this recipe it is pan-fried until crispy, then tossed with the dressing. Try to use mango that is ripe, yet firm enough to make it easy to chop.

1 Cut away the base and top third of the lemongrass, and slice the soft, inner part finely. Add the oil to a large, heavy-based sauté pan or wok, and heat to medium high. Add the lemongrass and fry for about 2 minutes, stirring, until soft.

2 Turn the heat up high, add the pork mince, and cook until crispy and brown underneath before breaking it up with a fork. Stir in the sugar and continue to fry, stirring, for about 5 minutes, until thoroughly cooked through. Remove from the heat and set aside.

3 Pour the dressing over the pork, add the onion, mango, and coriander, then stir gently to combine. Use the baby lettuce leaves as serving bowls or to scoop up the meat.

Prepare ahead
Prepare the ingredients and the dressing on the morning of serving. Dress the pork while warm about 1 hour before serving.

INGREDIENTS

3 stalks lemongrass

2 tbsp vegetable oil

400g (14oz) lean pork mince

1 tbsp soft brown sugar

1 recipe chilli lime dressing (*see p216*)

1 small red onion, finely diced

1 ripe but firm mango, diced

3 tbsp fresh chopped coriander

20 baby gem lettuce leaves, chilled, to serve

Preparation time 20 minutes
Cooking time 10 minutes
Makes 20 lettuce cups

BUY AND ARRANGE

Spicy peanut sauce (*see p218*) • prawn and cucumber skewers (*see p149*) • exotic fruit salad (*see p215*)

PARTNER WITH

Thai sweetcorn fritters (*see p26*) • seared sesame tuna (*see p138*) • grilled baby aubergines (*see p170*)

Colours

- Sky blue
- Mustard yellow
- French blue
- Delicate lavender
- Bone white

Tableware

- Distressed white china
- Bone-handled cutlery
- Yellow mimosa flowers
- Rustic terracotta plates
- Plain linen napkins

Mediterranean table

In the countries that sit along the Mediterranean Sea you will encounter people more passionate and spirited about food than perhaps those you meet anywhere else. It is paramount here, and life revolves around mealtimes. Of course, if we could all eat al fresco all year round, under the gently-soothing sun, we might quickly adjust our priorities too.

If you want to be assured of creating outstanding Mediterranean food, then it is important to track the seasons. Each brings its own fresh bounty: spring artichokes, summer tomatoes, autumn mushrooms, and bitter winter radicchio. Conveniently, grassy extra virgin olive oils, capers, anchovies, and nutty parmesan remain all year. Most herbs are embraced in Mediterranean cuisine; sage, basil, parsley, and dill all make an appearance, adding freshness and perfume.

To dress the table, opt for cheerful sky blue or earthy mustard linen cloths, rustic white or terracotta plates and bowls, and pleasantly-worn plain steel or bone-handled cutlery. Fill a large water pitcher or jug with fresh flowers, such as yellow mimosa, twist open a Campari soda, and bring the warmth and glow of Mediterranean sunshine into your home.

Flavours

- Grassy olive oil
- Sage, basil, parsley, and dill
- Salty capers and anchovies
- Fragrant cheeses
- Fresh lemon

Nibbles

- Marinated anchoives (*see p30*)
- Parmesan crisps (*see p31*)
- Prosciutto-wrapped melon (*see p31*)
- Roasted garlic with bread (*see p71*)
- Spanish or Italian deli plate (*see p30*)

Menu

Fried artichokes Roman style
with saffron aioli

Bresaola and pear rolls
with rocket and Parmesan

Three tomato salad
with goat's cheese and croûtons

Gorgonzola crostini
with garlic greens and sultanas

Rosemary lamb cutlets
with fresh mint and parsely sauce

Chocolate Frangelico pudding
with hazelnuts

BUY AND ARRANGE

Pesto and aioli with grissini
breadsticks (see p70)

Marinated green olives with celery
(see p30)

Prosciutto-wrapped melon (see p31)

Fried artichokes Roman style (see p12)

Bresaola and pear rolls (see p188)

Three tomato salad (see p86)

Gorgonzola crostini (see p166)

Rosemary lamb cutlets (see p118)

Chocolate Frangelic pudding (see p200)

Two days before
- Make croûtons for tomato salad
- Make base of crostini
- Marinate lamb cutlets
- Marinate green olives

The night before
- Prepare artichokes and leave to soak in lemon water
- Make saffron aioli
- Make chocolate Frangelico puddings

Four hours before
- Make bresaola and pear rolls
- Chop tomatoes for salad
- Make prosciutto-wrapped melon

Blood orange campari soda

Campari has a slightly bitter taste which mixes well with sweet blood orange juice and bubbly soda water. Italians are fond of it as a cool and refreshing aperitif.

INGREDIENTS

Ice

125ml (4fl oz) campari

570ml (1 pint) soda water

½ litre (17fl oz) blood orange juice or tangerine juice

1 orange, sliced, to garnish

Makes 4 cocktails

Half fill 4 tall highball glasses with ice. Pour the campari over, dividing it between the glasses. Add the blood orange juice and soda, again dividing them between the glasses. Decorate each glass with a slice of orange.

One hour before
- Remove olives from refrigerator
- Fry artichokes; keep warm in low oven
- Make greens for gorgonzola crostini
- Organize cocktail ingredients

At the last minute
- Plate artichokes with saffron aioli
- Plate bresaola and pear rolls
- Finish three tomato salad; plate
- Plate lamb cutlets with fresh mint and parsley sauce
- Plate prosciutto-wrapped melon
- Pour cocktails

Half an hour before
- Assemble tomato salad without basil and dressing
- Finish gorgonzola crostini; plate
- Sear lamb cutlets and keep warm under foil
- Plate pesto, aioli, and grissini breadsticks

Seared cinnamon duck
with mango chutney and poppadom

The duck in this recipe benefits vastly from overnight marinating; the process intensifies its flavour enormously. It is fine to buy your favourite chutney if you don't have time to make it yourself.

1 Cut a cross hatch pattern into the skin of the duck. Put it in a shallow bowl with all the marinade ingredients. Turn to coat, and leave to marinate for at least an hour, preferably overnight.

2 Preheat the oven to 200°C (400°F/Gas mark 6). Remove the duck from the marinade and drain on kitchen towel. Heat a non-stick frying pan to high, add the duck, fat-side down, and brown. Reduce the heat to low and melt the duck fat for about 5 minutes, until clear and very thin.

3 Place the duck in a small baking dish and roast in the oven for 10 minutes. Remove and leave to rest for 10 minutes on a cutting board, then slice very thinly. To serve, arrange the duck in small bowls with a spoonful of chutney, rocket, and pieces of poppadom, or slivers of naan bread.

Prepare ahead

The duck can be marinated for up to 2 days. If it is to be served cold, it can be cooked the day before serving. If it is to be eaten warm, it can be browned the day before. The chutney can be made a week in advance and refrigerated.

INGREDIENTS

2 duck breasts

1 recipe mango chutney (see p216), to serve

2 handfuls of rocket, to serve

Poppadoms or naan bread, to serve

Marinade

1 tbsp soy sauce

1 tsp honey

½ tsp Chinese five spice powder

½ tsp ground cinnamon

1cm (½in) piece root ginger, grated

½ tsp fresh cracked pepper

Preparation time 45 minutes, plus 1 hour to overnight marinating time

Cooking time 15 minutes

Makes 8 small servings

BUY AND ARRANGE

Raita with naan bread (see p71) • selection of chutneys and pickles (see p70) • spice-dusted prawns (see p148)

PARTNER WITH

Coconut prawns (see p14) • halibut parcels (see p146) • pea and prawn samosas (see p194)

Sticky chicken wings
in teriyaki sauce

Try to buy organic chicken since it will have more flavour. The wings are easier to eat if they're cut in half, but if you're not confident doing this, have your butcher take care of it.

1 To make the teriyaki sauce, place all of the ingredients in a saucepan and heat until the sugar is dissolved. Transfer to a large bowl.

2 Take each chicken wing and snap back each joint. Using a pair of poultry scissors or a cleaver, cut through the knuckle and separate into two pieces. Add the chicken to the teriyaki sauce, cover, and leave to marinate overnight in the refrigerator.

3 Preheat the oven to 180°C (350°F/Gas mark 4). Remove the wings from the marinade and place them on a non-stick baking sheet. Cover with foil and roast for 30 minutes. Remove the foil and roast for a further 15 minutes, until glossy and crispy at the edges.

Prepare ahead

The marinade can be made 1 week ahead and refrigerated.
The wings can be marinated for up to 72 hours before cooking.

INGREDIENTS

2.3kg (5lb) chicken wings

Sauce
60ml (2fl oz) dark soy sauce
60ml (2fl oz) sake
2 tbsp mirin
5 tbsp sugar
125ml (4fl oz) apricot juice
1 tbsp grated root ginger
2 garlic cloves, finely chopped
1 tsp Tabasco sauce
Juice of ½ lemon
2 tbsp rice vinegar

Preparation time 15 minutes, plus overnight marinating time
Cooking time 45 minutes
Makes 30 wings

BUY AND ARRANGE

Steamed edamame (see p173) • freshly sliced watermelon (see p215) • prawn and cucumber skewers (see p149)

PARTNER WITH

Saffron coconut soup (see p42) • miso halibut bites (see p140) • glass noodle salad (see p76)

Hainanese chicken
with sweet soy and chilli dipping sauce

This recipe is based on a classic Chinese dish, which features a whole bird poached. This is a bite-sized variation enlivened with cucumber ribbons and crunchy lettuce.

1 In a saucepan, bring the stock to the boil, add the chicken breasts and poach for 5 minutes. Turn off the heat and place a lid on the saucepan. Leave the chicken to rest for 30 minutes.

2 Drain the chicken, transfer to a chopping board, and cut into thin slices. Using the lettuce leaves as cups, fill with the chicken, cucumber, spring onions, and coriander, and garnish with red chilli. Serve with the sweet soy and chilli dipping sauce.

Prepare ahead

The sauce can be made 1 day in advance. The chicken can be poached on the morning of serving and kept refrigerated.

INGREDIENTS

600ml (1 pint) chicken stock

4 boneless skinless chicken breasts

20–25 baby gem or cos lettuce, chilled for serving

2 Lebanese or other small cucumbers, thinly sliced lengthways

4 spring onions, very thinly sliced lengthways

1 small handful fresh coriander, roughly chopped

1 red chilli, thinly sliced, to garnish

1 recipe sweet soy and chilli dipping sauce (see p218), to serve

Preparation time 10 minutes
Cooking time 5 minutes, plus 30 minutes resting
Makes 20–25 small portions

BUY AND ARRANGE

Steamed edamame (see p173)
• spicy peanut dip (see p71)
• fresh oysters on the shell (see p148)

PARTNER WITH

Crispy scallops (see p24) • pork and prawn dumplings (see p184) • coconut macaroons (see p210)

Seared beef carpaccio
with mustard mint sauce and rocket

Carpaccio is simple to make at home and perfect for preparing in advance. I've suggested a larger piece of beef than you'll need because it is much easier to slice in this quantity. Use what is leftover as a tasty sandwich filling.

1   Preheat a non-stick frying pan. Brush the meat with 2 tablespoons of olive oil, and sprinkle with the salt and pepper. Place in the pan and brown quickly on all sides. Remove and tightly wrap with plastic wrap to create as round a shape as possible. Place in the freezer for 1–2 hours.

2   Meanwhile, to make the sauce, place all of the ingredients in a small bowl and whisk until thoroughly combined.

3   Using a very sharp meat knife, slice the semi-frozen meat into 8 slices, about 6mm (¼in) thick. Place each slice between two pieces of greaseproof paper. Gently pound the beef with a meat tenderizer or with the side of a rolling pin, avoiding tearing. Place one slice in a shallow glass dish. Drizzle with olive oil and sprinkle with salt and coarsely ground black pepper. Repeat with the remaining slices. Refrigerate until serving.

4   Carefully arrange the meat on a platter or on individual plates. Spoon the sauce to one side and sprinkle with capers. Garnish with the Parmesan and rocket.

Prepare ahead
Both the beef and the sauce can be prepared on the morning of serving, covered, and kept in the refrigerator until ready to serve.

INGREDIENTS

250g (8oz) beef fillet, trimmed of all fat and sinew

2 tbsp extra virgin olive oil, plus extra for drizzling

½ tsp each salt and pepper

1 tbsp small capers, rinsed

25g (1oz) Parmesan, shaved into thin curls

2 large handfuls of rocket leaves

Sauce

1 tbsp Dijon mustard

1 tbsp chopped mint leaves

2 tbsp extra virgin olive oil

1 tbsp balsamic vinegar

Preparation time 20 minutes, plus 1–2 hours freezing time

Makes 8 small servings

BUY AND ARRANGE

Fig, prosciutto, and mozzarella salad (see p92) • marinated Italian mushrooms (see p172) • marinated anchovies (see p30)

PARTNER WITH

Fried artichokes Roman style (see p12) • spiced goat's cheese balls (see p59) • creamy celery and fennel soup (see p34)

Tandoori chicken thighs
with tomato and coconut sambal

Many tandoori restaurants use food colouring in this dish. However, once you have made this homemade version, you will see that such artifice isn't necessary.

1 Cut 3 slashes across the top of each chicken thigh. Combine all of the remaining ingredients, except the sambal, together in a shallow glass dish. Add the chicken, turn to coat, and marinate for at least 4 hours, but preferably overnight.

2 Preheat the oven to its highest setting. Remove the chicken from the marinade, spread it out on a large, non-stick baking sheet, and cook for 30 minutes, until crispy around the edges. Alternatively cook under a very hot grill or on a barbecue. Serve with the tomato and coconut sambal.

Prepare ahead

The chicken should, if possible, be marinated overnight. It can be partially roasted in the oven for about 20 minutes, refrigerated, and then finished for a further 10 minutes before serving. The tomato and coconut sambal can be made 4 hours in advance.

INGREDIENTS

8 large chicken thighs with bone (skinless, if you prefer)

100g (4oz) yoghurt

3 garlic cloves, crushed

1 tsp garam masala

Juice of ½ lemon

1 tbsp grated root ginger

1 tsp ground coriander

1 tsp chilli powder

1 tbsp ground cumin

1 recipe tomato and coconut sambal (see p92), to serve

Preparation time 10 minutes, plus 4 hours marinating time

Cooking time 30 minutes

Makes 8 thighs

BUY AND ARRANGE

Selection of chutneys and pickles (see p70) • unshelled pistachios (see p31)

PARTNER WITH

Tomato and ginger soup (see p50) • pea and prawn samosas (see p194) • seared cinnamon duck (see p124)

Sage and lemon meatballs
with Parmesan

Using veal allows you to make the most featherweight, juicy meatballs, but if you don't like to use it, you can substitute minced pork instead.

1 Preheat the oven to 200°C (400°F/Gas mark 6). Place the bread in a large mixing bowl with the milk and leave to soak until softened. Add the meat, sage, fennel seed, garlic, lemon zest, tomatoes, Parmesan, egg, salt, and pepper. Mix well with your hands and shape into 2.5cm (1in) meatballs.

2 Heat the oil in a non-stick frying pan to medium high. Fry the balls in batches of 5–6 for 5 minutes, until browned on all sides. Shake the pan frequently to keep them from sticking. Drain on kitchen towel and place in the oven while cooking the other batches. Serve on the radicchio leaves with the vinegar for dipping.

Prepare ahead

The meatballs can be made the day before and reheated in an oven preheated to 200°C (400°F/Gas mark 6) for 4 minutes, or until warmed through. Alternatively they can be frozen raw or partially cooked, defrosted, then cooked before eating.

INGREDIENTS

2 slices white bread, crusts removed

60ml (2fl oz) milk

500g (1lb) veal or pork mince

15g (½oz) fresh sage, finely chopped

1 tsp fennel seed, crushed

1 garlic clove, finely chopped

Grated zest of 1 lemon

2 sundried tomatoes in oil, finely chopped

60g (1oz) Parmesan, grated

1 egg, beaten

½ tsp each salt and pepper

2 tbsp olive oil

Radicchio leaves, pre-soaked for 1 hour in iced water to remove bitterness, to serve

Balsamic vinegar, for dipping

Preparation time 15 minutes
Cooking time 35 minutes
Makes 35 meatballs

BUY AND ARRANGE

Radishes with tapenade (see p173) • chicory salad (see p93) • gorgonzola crostini (see p31)

PARTNER WITH

Chunky aubergine sticks (see p23) • bagna cauda dip (see p54) • three tomato salad (see p86)

Five spice hoisin ribs
with spring onions

Slow cooking makes the pork wonderfully tender, nearly to the point of melting off the bones. If you prefer, ask your butcher to prepare the spare ribs for you.

1 Preheat the oven to 140°C (275°F/Gas mark 1). Rub the ribs with the five spice powder and season. Divide between 2 non-stick roasting trays, cover tightly with foil, and cook for 1 hour.

2 Meanwhile, to make the sauce, heat the oil in a wok until hot and add the ginger and garlic. Fry for 1 minute, then add all of the remaining sauce ingredients. Remove the ribs from the oven and mix well with the sauce. Return to the oven and cook, covered, for 30 minutes. Remove the foil and complete cooking for a final 30 minutes. Serve on plates, garnished with the spring onion.

Prepare ahead

The ribs can be cooked on the morning of serving and then reheated for 5 minutes in an oven preheated to 200°C (400°F/Gas mark 6).

INGREDIENTS

1.5kg (3.3lb) pork spare ribs, cut into single ribs and halved

1 tsp five spice powder

5 spring onions, finely shredded, to garnish

Sauce

3 tbsp groundnut oil

2 tsp grated root ginger

2 garlic cloves, crushed

60ml (2fl oz) hoisin sauce

2 tbsp soy sauce

2 tbsp bottled sweet chilli dipping sauce

60ml (2fl oz) honey

75g (2½oz) soft brown sugar

75ml (2½fl oz) dry sherry

Preparation time 15 minutes
Cooking time 2 hours
Makes about 30 ribs

BUY AND ARRANGE

Watercress salad with spring onion (*see p93*) • roasted asparagus with soy (*see p172*) • selection of sushi (*see p30*)

PARTNER WITH

Thai sweetcorn fritters (*see p26*) • glass noodle salad (*see p76*) • avocado crostini (*see p164*)

No need to be shy; cooking fish and seafood isn't as scary as you might think. Find some exceptionally fresh fish, a fishmonger who is happy to put in the hard work, and you are all set. Steamed, roasted, grilled, or sushi-style, eating fish is a delicate and special pleasure.

Fish

Baby clams
with sherry and caramelized onions

Oloroso is a dry, raisin-scented sherry, with a slightly smoky taste. It is wonderful to cook with as well as to sip chilled. Cockles may be used instead of baby clams in this recipe.

1 To draw out any sand from inside the clams, soak them fully immersed in cold water with a handful of salt for 30 minutes. Rinse the clams, wrap in a wet tea towel, place in a bowl and refrigerate until using. Discard any clams with open shells.

2 Put the oil in a medium-sized saucepan, add the onions, salt and pepper, and sauté for 10–12 minutes, until the onions are caramelized. Add the garlic and ham, and sauté for a further 3 minutes, until soft. Stir in the sherry and cook for 1–2 minutes.

3 Just before serving, add the clams to the pan: they should open in about 1–2 minutes. Discard any that do not open. Sprinkle with parsley and serve with crostini.

Prepare ahead

The sauce may be prepared on the morning of serving, and the prepared clams added and cooked just before serving.

INGREDIENTS

1kg (2.2lb) baby clams, cleaned and beards removed

3 tbsp olive oil

2 yellow onions, finely sliced

½ tsp each salt and pepper

2 garlic cloves, finely chopped

6 slices of serrano ham or proscuitto, chopped

125ml (4fl oz) oloroso or manzanilla sherry

Small handful flat-leaf parsley, finely chopped

8 slices sourdough bread, toasted, rubbed with garlic and olive oil, to serve

Preparation time 10 minutes, plus 30 minutes soaking time

Cooking time 20 minutes

Makes 8 small bowls of clams

BUY AND ARRANGE

Radicchio, orange, and rocket salad (*see p92*) • roasted garlic with warm bread (*see p71*) • pan-fried chorizo (*see p149*)

PARTNER WITH

Pan-fried halloumi salad (*see p82*) • fried artichokes Roman style (*see p12*) • chocolate Frangelico pudding (*see p200*)

Seared sesame tuna
with sweet soy and chilli dressing

Making seared rare tuna is very easy. Just be sure to buy good quality fish - ruby red with a little white marbling throughout – and do not overcook it.

1 Cut the tuna lengthways into 2–3 long slices, 5cm (2in) wide, like small beef fillets. Heat a large, non-stick sauté pan on a medium high heat. Meanwhile, rub the tuna fillets with the olive oil and then roll in the salt, pepper, and sesame seeds. Place the fillets in the dry pan and sear until brown on all sides. Be sure not to overcook, as the meat should be rare inside.

2 Allow the tuna to cool slightly, then wrap it very tightly in plastic wrap. The more tightly it is wrapped, the firmer it will be to slice. Refrigerate for at least 1 hour and preferably overnight.

3 Unwrap the fish and slice very thinly, about 5mm (¼in) thick. Arrange a bed of spring onions, apple, and cucumber on individual plates, and top with the tuna. Serve accompanied by the sweet soy and chilli dressing.

Prepare ahead

The fish is best prepared the night before so that it is very firm to cut. The dressing can be made and the vegetables and fruit sliced on the morning of serving. Keep the onions and apples in iced water to prevent discolouring and drain before serving.

INGREDIENTS

750g (1½lb) fresh tuna, preferably tail

1 tbsp olive oil

½ tsp each salt and pepper

1 tsp each black sesame seeds and white sesame seeds

4 spring onions, cut into matchsticks

1 granny smith, or any apple, cut into matchsticks

1 cucumber, cut into matchsticks

1 recipe sweet soy and chilli dressing (*see p218*), to serve

Preparation time 15 minutes, plus 1–12 hours refrigeration for the tuna

Cooking time 5 minutes

Makes 8 small starters

BUY AND ARRANGE

Watercress salad with spring onion (*see p93*) • crab and cream cheese dip (*see p71*) • mango fool (*see p215*)

PARTNER WITH

Peking seared duck rolls (*see p180*) • sticky chicken wings (*see p126*) • avocado crostini (*see p164*)

Halibut bites
with sticky miso glaze

Other fish, such as scallops, monkfish, or firm cod fillets can be used instead. The saltiness of the light miso paste preserves the fish while it is marinating.

1 To make the glaze, mix the mirin, miso paste, sake, and sugar in a small bowl. Add the fish and turn to coat thoroughly. Cover and leave to marinate in the refrigerator for at least 24 hours.

2 Preheat the grill to medium. Place the fish on a roasting tray fitted with a flat rack. Grill for about 4–5 minutes, until golden and crispy around the edges. Sprinkle with the spring onions and serve warm with chopsticks or toothpicks.

Prepare ahead

The fish can be marinated 24–48 hours before serving. It should be grilled just before serving and eaten immediately.

INGREDIENTS

500g (1lb) halibut, cleaned of all sinew and cut into 4cm (1½in) chunks

3 spring onions, with green stems, sliced lengthways

Glaze

75ml (3fl oz) mirin

200g (7oz) light miso paste

3 tbsp sake

125g (4oz) caster sugar

Preparation time 15 minutes plus 24 hours marinating time

Cooking time 5 minutes

Makes about 30 bites

BUY AND ARRANGE

Prawn and cucumber skewers (see p149) • crab and cream cheese dip (see p71) • watercress salad with spring onion (see p93)

PARTNER WITH

Roasted butternut squash (see p162) • crispy scallops (see p24) • seared sesame tuna (see p138)

Grilled butterflied prawns
with butter, lime, and jalapeño

Cooking prawns with their shells on keeps them succulent and juicy. Not only do larger prawns look more impressive, but it is also easier to butterfly them.

1 Using a very sharp knife, cut each prawn through the shell on the back (outside curve). Don't cut all the way through, but just enough to split the prawn open; this is butterflying. Rinse under cold water to remove any veins. Drain on kitchen towel.

2 Heat the grill to medium. Place the prawns in a shallow baking dish and pour over the butter and oil. Sprinkle with the garlic, chipotle, jalapeño, salt, and pepper. Cook under the grill for 1–2 minutes, or until the prawns just turn pink. Sprinkle with the lime juice, zest, and fresh coriander and serve immediately with the lime halves.

Prepare ahead
The butter can be mixed with the chillies 2 days in advance, refrigerated, and melted before cooking. The prawns can be butterflied the night before and refrigerated.

INGREDIENTS

500g (1lb) large prawns in shells

30g (1oz) unsalted butter, melted

2 tbsp extra virgin olive oil

2 garlic cloves, crushed

1 chipotle chilli in adobo, de-seeded and chopped (or extra jalapeño or green chilli)

1 jalapeño or other green chilli, de-seeded and minced

½ tsp each salt and pepper

Juice of 1 large lime

1 tsp lime zest

3 tbsp chopped fresh coriander

2 limes, halved, to serve

Preparation time 25 minutes
Cooking time 2 minutes
Makes about 20–24 prawns

BUY AND ARRANGE

Palm heart and avocado salad (see p92) • sweet potato wedges (see p172) • baby lettuce with walnut oil and sherry vinegar (see p92)

PARTNER WITH

Crab and gruyére nachos (see p142) • soft shell steak tacos (see p178) • chilli gazpacho (see p36)

Crab and gruyère nachos
with charred tomato salsa

A plate of nachos rarely sits uneaten. There's something irresistible about melted cheese. Instead of the chipotle, you can use another red chilli or jalapeño chilli.

1　To make the salsa, place the garlic cloves and chillies in a non-stick frying pan and dry-fry, stirring, until blackened on all sides. Remove from the heat and set the garlic aside. Place the chillies in a plastic bag, seal, and leave for 5 minutes to steam. Scrape off the skins and take the seeds out. Peel the cooled garlic.

2　Meanwhile, heat the grill to high. Spread out the tomatoes and onion on a large, non-stick baking sheet and grill for 6–7 minutes, until blackened. Transfer to a food processor with the garlic, chillies, the chipotle in adobo, if using, and the coriander and salt. Pulse until you have a coarse-textured purée. Transfer to a bowl and add the lime juice and extra salt to taste, if necessary.

3　Preheat the oven to 200°C (400°F/Gas mark 6). Spread the nachos out on the baking sheet. Sprinkle with the crab, pickled jalapeño, onion, and cheese. Bake for 6 minutes, until the cheese is melted. Serve immediately with the salsa.

Prepare ahead

The vegetables and cheese can be chopped and grated in the morning. The nachos can be assembled 1 hour before baking.

INGREDIENTS

1 x 200g (7oz) bag very good-quality corn nachos

250g (8oz) cooked fresh white crab meat

1 pickled jalapeño, very thinly sliced

1 small red onion, finely diced

250g (8oz), finely grated Gruyère or mature Cheddar

Salsa

4 garlic cloves, unpeeled

2 jalapeño or other small green chillies

500g (1lb) ripe plum tomatoes

1 red onion, thickly sliced

1 chipotle in adobo, de-seeded (*optional*)

Small handful fresh coriander

½ tsp salt

Juice of 1 lime

Preparation time 20 minutes
Cooking time 16 minutes
Makes 8 servings

BUY AND ARRANGE	PARTNER WITH
Watermelon and feta salad (*see p93*) • piquillo peppers with sherry vinegar (*see p172*) • Spanish deli plate (*see p30*)	Soft shell steak tacos (*see p178*) • baby clams (*see p136*) • chilli gazpacho (*see p36*) • chocolate cupcakes (*see p202*)

Smoked trout carpaccio
with pink peppercorns and dill

You can make this with any thinly sliced smoked fish.
Instead of trout, try smoked salmon, tuna, or swordfish,
but leave the challenge of slicing it to your fishmonger.

1 Divide the fish slices between individual plates and drizzle with
the olive oil. Sprinkle with the fennel, onion, peppercorns, capers,
and dill.

2 Just before serving, spoon over the crème fraîche and place
some rocket and a lemon or lime wedge on each plate.

Prepare ahead
This dish can be made on the morning of serving, covered
with plastic wrap, and refrigerated until ready to serve.

INGREDIENTS

250g (8oz) smoked trout slices

2 tbsp extra virgin olive oil

½ fennel bulb, core removed
and finely diced

1 small red onion, finely diced

2 tbsp pink peppercorns,
crushed

1 tbsp tiny capers

Small bunch of fresh dill, stems
removed and leaves chopped

100g (3oz) crème fraîche

Small handful rocket

Lemons or limes, quartered,
to serve

Preparation time 15 minutes
Makes 8 small plates

BUY AND ARRANGE

Chicory salad (*see p93*) •
gorgonzola crostini (*see p31*) •
biscotti, mascapone, and
dessert wine (*see p215*)

PARTNER WITH

Mushroom and chestnut
soup (*see p38*) • rosemary
lamb chops (*see p118*) •
baby beetroot and bresaola
(*see p168*)

Roasted prawns and tomatoes
with gremolata

Butterflying prawns creates a more elegant presentation and it prevents them from curling. Have plenty of crusty bread available to soak up the delicious sauce.

1 Preheat the oven to 180°C (350°F/Gas mark 4). Place the tomatoes, cut side up, on a baking tray, and sprinkle with the garlic, chillies, olive oil, salt, and pepper. Bake for 20 minutes.

2 Remove the tomatoes from the oven and add the prawns, fennel seed, and lemon juice. Heat the grill to medium and grill the prawn and tomato mixture for 4–5 minutes, until the prawns turn white. Divide between individual plates, sprinkle with the parsley and lemon zest and serve warm, or at room temperature.

Prepare ahead

The tomatoes can be roasted on the morning of serving and the other ingredients chopped. If serving at room temperature, the dish may be fully made 2 hours before.

INGREDIENTS

250g (8oz) baby or very small plum tomatoes, halved

2 garlic cloves, finely chopped

½ tsp crushed, dried red chillies

4 tbsp extra virgin olive oil

½ tsp each salt and pepper

500g (1lb) prawns, peeled, de-veined, and butterflied (*see p141*)

½ tsp fennel seed, crushed

Juice and grated zest of 1 lemon

3 tbsp flat-leaf parsley, finely chopped

Preparation time 10 minutes
Cooking time 5 minutes
Makes 8 servings

BUY AND ARRANGE

Pesto and aioli with grissini breadsticks (*see p70*) • marinated anchovies (*see p30*) • pan-fried padron peppers (*see p30*)

PARTNER WITH

Farro salad (*see p78*) • artichoke puff pastry bites (*see p196*) • strawberries and figs (*see p207*)

Halibut parcels
with coriander and coconut chutney

Find the freshest, preferably organic, coconuts to use in this recipe. However, quality dried coconut can still be amazingly good. Try salmon or seabass in the recipe instead.

1 Preheat the oven to 200°C (400°F/Gas mark 6). To make the chutney, heat a small, non-stick frying pan, add the cumin seeds and dry toast, stirring. Cool and grind in a spice mill or mortar. Reserve a little coriander as a garnish, and place the remainder in a food processor or blender with the garlic, ginger, chilli, and lemon juice. Process to a paste. Transfer to a small bowl and stir in the coconut, toasted cumin seeds, and sugar.

2 Cut 8 large pieces of foil. Put a small knob of the butter on each piece. Top with 2 tablespoons of chutney, then a piece of fish, and finally a further 2 tablespoons chutney, then season. Fold the foil around the fish to create sealed packets, place on a baking sheet then bake in the oven for 10 minutes, or until the fish is tender and can be pierced with a knife. Open the packets, garnish with the reserved coriander, and serve with lemon wedges.

Prep ahead

Both the parcels and chutney can be made on the morning of serving and be kept refrigerated.

INGREDIENTS

750g (1½lb) halibut, skinned, boned, cut in 8 pieces

60g (2oz) unsalted butter

Salt and pepper

1 lemon, cut into wedges

Chutney

1 tsp cumin seeds

1 large bunch of fresh coriander

2 garlic cloves

2½cm (1in) piece of ginger, peeled and sliced

1 green chilli, seeded and chopped

Juice of 2 lemons

250g (8oz) grated fresh or desiccated unsweetened coconut (organic if possible)

2 tsp sugar

Preparation time 15 minutes
Cooking time 10 minutes
Makes 8 parcels

BUY AND ARRANGE

Selection of chutneys and pickles (*see p70*) • raita with naan bread (*see p71*) • spice-dusted prawns (*see p148*)

PARTNER WITH

Tomato and ginger soup (*see p50*) • crispy vegetable pakoras (*see p20*) • strawberries and figs (*see p207*)

Quick fish and meat
buy and arrange ideas for quick-to-prepare dishes

Fish and meat dishes are considered to be complicated and fiddly to make, but there are some clever shortcuts that will save you time. Fresh fish needs little added to it, tasting wonderful with just a little lemon juice or seasoning. The chorizo and mergez sausages are simply pan-fried – and impossible to resist.

Fresh crab crostini
Toast 16 small slices of French or sourdough bread and brush each with some olive oil. In a bowl, mix together 200g (7oz) fresh cooked white crab meat, juice of ½ a lemon, a pinch of crushed chillis, 2 tablespoons extra virgin olive oil, and some seasoning. Top each crostini with a good portion of the crab mixture.

Spice-dusted prawns
Butterfly 16 large, peeled prawns by slicing a deep cut down the back. Open them out flat so they resemble a butterfly and rinse them under water. Place either some ground fennel, ground cumin, ground coriander, or sumac, in a bowl. Dip each prawn into the bowl so that it is fully coated, then season. Heat 1 tablespoon olive oil in a non-stick frying pan and fry the prawns until just opaque, about 3 minutes. Serve on a platter.

Smoked salmon blinis
Buy some ready-made blinis and bake them until crisp in a moderately hot oven. Top each blini with some small strips of smoked salmon, a few capers, a spoonful of crème fraîche, some finely diced red onion, and a little freshly chopped dill. Serve them on a platter.

Fresh oysters on the shell
Ask a fishmonger to open the oysters for you, or if you wish to open them yourself, take care and use the correct knife and gloves. Place the oysters, still in their opened shell, on a bed of ice on a small tray and serve them with some Tabasco sauce and lemon wedges for guests to add as they require. Alternatively, in a small serving bowl, mix together 5 tablespoons rice wine vinegar and 1 small diced chilli and allow guests to sprinkle about ½ teaspoon of the mixture over their oyster before eating.

Tuna tartare on cucumber slices
In a bowl, combine 125g (4oz) finely diced raw tuna with 1 teaspoon lime juice, ½ teaspoon wasabi, and 1 teaspoon soy. Slice 1 medium cucumber thinly and serve 1 heaped teaspoon of the tuna mixture on each.

Gravadlax and mustard dill sauce
Buy some quality gravadlax salmon from a delicatessen or supermarket. In a bowl, mix 4 tablespoons Dijon mustard, 1 teaspoon sugar, 1 tablespoon chopped dill and 1 tablespoon white wine vinegar. Serve the gravadlax with the dip and some toasted dark or seeded bread.

Prawn and cucumber skewers

Cut 1 medium cucumber into 2cm (¾in) cubes. Feed 1 large cooked prawn and 1 cucumber cube onto each skewer. Alternatively use slender forks or toothpicks. Serve the skewers with a bowl of hoisin sauce or ketchup manis, also known as Indonesian sweet soy, to dip.

Pan-fried chorizo

Cut some chorizo into 1.5cm (½in) pieces or buy smaller chorizos and use them whole. Heat a little olive oil in a non-stick frying pan until hot. Add the chorizo to the pan and fry until crispy, about 2 minutes. Remove them with a slotted spoon and drain on kitchen towel, then serve.

Five spice chicken breast bites

Cut 3 skinless boneless chicken breasts into 2.5cm (1in) pieces. Place some five spice powder in a bowl. Roll the chicken pieces in the powder, then season with salt. Heat 1 tablespoon vegetable oil in a non-stick pan and brown the chicken on all sides, about 5 minutes. Serve with lime wedges, chilli dipping sauce, and some toothpicks to pick them up.

Baby prawns with rocket

Place 250g (8oz) small, cooked prawns on a serving dish. Scatter over 2 large handfuls of rocket and drizzle with 1 tablespoon extra virgin olive oil. Serve with some lemon wedges to squeeze over, if desired.

Prawn and cucumber skewers

Pan-fried Merquez lamb sausages

Heat 1 tablespoon olive oil in a non-stick frying pan until hot. Add the sausages and pan-fry them, turning occasionally, until golden and cooked through. Slice the sausages into smaller pieces, if desired, and serve with toothpicks.

Thai prawns

In a large bowl, place some large, cooked and peeled prawns, about 250g (8oz), 4 tablespoons sweet chilli dipping sauce, and 1 small handful chopped fresh coriander, and mix well to coat the prawns. Serve them on small skewers or with toothpicks for guests to help themselves.

Choice is not an issue with fresh vegetables. From autumn's crimson beetroot to spring's emerald asparagus, each season brings a rich new selection. There are endless ways to prepare them, and simple is usually best. Often, all that's called for is a hint of garlic, seasoning, lemon juice, or creamy goat's cheese.

Vegetables

Serrano-rolled asparagus
with saffron aioli

Tasty on its own or divine with a dipping sauce, this undemanding asparagus dish works well for Moorish and Mediterranean menus.

1 Bring a saucepan of salted water to the boil, add the asparagus, and simmer for 1–2 minutes. Remove with tongs, and immediately plunge into iced water to retain the colour and halt their cooking. Drain on a tea towel.

2 Roll two spears of asparagus in one piece of ham. Repeat with the remaining asparagus and ham. Refrigerate until ready to serve with the saffron aioli.

Prepare ahead
The asparagus can be blanched and rolled on the morning of serving, covered with parchment paper and then plastic wrap. The aioli can be made the day before. Both should be refrigerated.

INGREDIENTS

2 bunches asparagus, ends trimmed

12 slices Serrano ham, bresaola or prosciutto, cut in half

1 recipe saffron lemon aioli (see p217), to serve

Preparation time 20 minutes
Cooking time 2 minutes
Makes 24 asparagus

BUY AND ARRANGE

Baby lettuces with sherry vinegar and walnut oil (see p92) • sweet potato wedges (see p172) • houmous with smoky paprika (see p70)

PARTNER WITH

Citrus swordfish brochettes (see p96) • chickpea and chilli dip (see p68) • chilli gazpacho (see p36)

Wild mushroom crostini
with mascapone and sherry vinegar

When making the crostini, try to bake the bread until it is browned at the edges but still chewy in the centre.

1 Preheat the oven to 200°C (400°F/Gas mark 6). Place the bread on a non-stick baking sheet, brush with the oil and sprinkle with salt. Bake for 6 minutes. Rub the bread with the whole garlic clove, then chop it for the topping and leave the bread to cool.

2 For the topping, heat the oil in a pan and sauté the garlic for 1 minute. Add the mushrooms and salt, toss gently to coat. Sauté for 4 minutes, until just wilting. Add the vinegar and parsley, toss gently, and remove from heat. Spread 1 tablespoon of mascapone on each crostini, spoon over the mixture, and sprinkle with zest.

Prepare ahead

Store toasted crostini in an airtight container 2 days ahead. Sauté mushrooms and refrigerate 2 hours before serving. Reheat or bring to room temperature and make crostini half an hour before serving.

INGREDIENTS

16 slices sourdough, ciabatta, or other artisan stick bread

3 tbsp extra virgin olive oil

Topping

3 tbsp extra virgin olive oil

2 garlic cloves, peeled and 1 finely chopped

500g (1lb) mixed wild mushrooms, such as girolles, trompettes de la mort, or chanterelles, quartered or thickly sliced

¼ tsp salt

1 tbsp sherry vinegar

Small handful flat-leaf parsley, finely chopped

250g (8oz) mascarpone cheese

Finely pared zest of 1 orange

Preparation time 25 minutes
Cooking time 11 minutes
Serves 16 pieces

BUY AND ARRANGE

Palm heart and avocado salad (see p92) • roasted peppers with garlic (see p172) • Italian deli plate (see p30)

PARTNER WITH

Spinach and peppered pear salad (see p84)• Sicilian artichoke bottoms (see p154) • raspberry meringues (see p208)

Sicilian artichoke bottoms
with provolone and capers

Preparing an artichoke bottom is easier than with hearts, which require more effort. Any type of bread is fine for the topping, but I find sourdough works well.

1 Preheat the oven to 200°C (400°F/Gas mark 6). Peel the outer leaves off one artichoke until you reach the pale green soft part. Slice off the stem. Using a heavy, sharp knife, cut away the top three-quarters of the artichoke, reserving the bottom. Trim off the hard edges with a smaller paring knife. Using a spoon, scrape out any remaining inner choke. Place the artichoke in a bowl of water with a third of the lemon juice. Repeat with the other artichokes.

2 Add 2 chopped garlic cloves and 3 tablespoons of the oil to a very large saucepan and sauté the garlic until slightly golden. Drain the artichokes, add to the pan, and cook for 1 minute, then add the mint, ½ teaspoon each of salt and pepper, the water, and the remaining lemon juice. Reduce the heat to medium low and cover the saucepan. Cook the artichokes for 10 minutes or until they can be pierced with a knife, but not mushy. Remove from the liquid and place on a non-stick baking tray.

3 In a small bowl, combine the breadcrumbs, lemon zest, parsley, capers, and the remaining garlic, olive oil, salt, and pepper. Place one slice of cheese on each artichoke bottom and distribute the breadcrumb mixture evenly on top of each. Bake in the oven for 15 minutes or until the cheese has melted and the breadcrumbs are toasty. Serve warm, garnished with the zest and rocket sprigs

Prepare ahead

The artichokes can be trimmed and poached the day before, then covered and refrigerated. The topping can also be made the day before and kept in the refrigerator.

INGREDIENTS

6–8 globe artichokes

Juice of 3 lemons

4 garlic cloves, chopped

6 tbsp olive oil

3 tbsp chopped fresh mint

1 tsp each salt and pepper

4 tbsp water

90g (3oz) home-made breadcrumbs

1 tsp grated lemon zest

3 tsp finely chopped flat-leaf parsley

1 tbsp small capers, rinsed

50g (2oz) or 6–8 slices of provolone cheese

Pared lemon zest, to garnish

Rocket, to garnish

Preparation time 45 minutes
Cooking time 25 minutes
Makes 6–8 bites

BUY AND ARRANGE

Radicchio, orange, and rocket salad (see p92) • prosciutto-wrapped melon (see p31) • marinated anchovies (see p30)

PARTNER WITH

Orange and beetroot soup (see p40) • three tomato salad (see p86) • seared beef carpaccio (see p128)

Colours
- Magenta pink
- Silver and gold
- Warm tangerine
- Rich purple
- Crimson red

Tableware
- Mixed styles of metal bowls
- Silk tablecloths
- Small wooden spice bowls
- Distressed metal cutlery
- Scattered rose petals

Bollywood nights

Indian cuisine is about glamour; redolent with heady spices, creamy with the texture of coconut, and brightened by the taste of sweet mango. Unique for the many fried snacks served with refreshing yoghurt dips, Indian food is a delight for your senses.

Garlic, fresh coriander, and ginger form the base of most dishes, and it is a great combination. Cardamom, cumin, and coriander may already be familiar spices, but there is more. Once you are exposed to the fascinating taste of amchoor, you'll understand the real meaning of exotic. Made from ground dried mango, amchoor adds a gentle sour note to samosas and other foods. Boredom will never be an issue when exploring this cuisine; there is so much to discover.

When setting the table, imagine colourful saris of magenta, orange, and silver. Don't try to be quietly tasteful, think electric bright colours – beige definitely does not belong here. Metal serving dishes and wooden spice bowls add an authentic touch, if you have them. Light some candles for atmosphere and prepare to feast.

Flavours

- Spicy chilli
- Fresh coriander
- Sweet garlic
- Sour amchoor
- Fragrant turmeric

Nibbles

- Raita with naan bread (see p71)
- Chutneys and pickles (see p70)
- Crispy vegetable pakoras (see p20)
- Sugar-coated fennel seeds (see p215)
- Tomato and coconut sambal (see p92)

Menu

Seared cinnamon duck
with mango chutney and poppadoms

Coconut prawns
with mango mint dipping sauce

Tomato and ginger soup
with spiced oil

Crispy vegetable pakoras with
tamarind and ginger dipping sauce

Tandoori chicken thighs
with tomato and coconut sambal

Raspberry meringues
with white chocolate swirls

BUY AND ARRANGE

Raita with naan bread
(see p71)

Selection of chutneys and pickles
with mini poppadoms *(see p70)*

Exotic fruit salad
(see p215)

Seared cinnamon duck
(see p124)

Coconut prawns
(see p14)

Tomato and ginger soup
(see p50)

Crispy vegetable pakoras
(see p20)

Tandoori chicken thighs
(see p130)

Raspberry meringues
(see p208)

The night before
- Marinate duck breasts
- Make mango chutney
- Make tomato and ginger soup
- Marinate tandoori chicken
- Make raspberry meringues

In the morning
- Sear duck breasts
- Make mango mint sauce
- Make tamarind and ginger sauce
- Whip cream and chop nuts for meringues
- Make iced chai tea
- Make raita

Four hours before
- Make crispy vegetable pakoras
- Roast tandoori chicken thighs
- Make tomato and coconut sambal
- Make exotic fruit salad

Iced chai tea with rose petals

This tea can be made into an alcoholic cocktail by adding a measure of vanilla vodka or brandy to each glass.

INGREDIENTS

2 litre (4¼ pints) boiling water

2 tbsp sugar

1 tsp rose water

8 chai tea bags

Ice

4 cinnamon sticks (*optional*)

Fresh red rose petals, to garnish

Makes 8 iced chai teas

Pour the boiling water into a large jug, then add the sugar, rose water, and tea bags. Allow it to steep for 5 minutes then remove the bags. Add some ice to cool the tea down. Fill each glass with more ice, pour the tea over, and add a cinnamon stick, if using. Scatter rose petals over the glasses and jug to garnish.

One hour before
- Coat coconut prawns
- Reheat soup and make spiced oil

At the last minute
- Plate coconut prawns with mango mint sauce
- Pour soup with spiced oil
- Reheat pakoras; plate with tamarind dipping sauce
- Plate raspberry meringues
- Pour iced chai tea
- Plate exotic fruit salad

Half an hour before
- Roast duck breasts; plate with chutney and poppadoms
- Fry coconut prawns
- Reheat tandoori chicken; plate
- Plate chutneys and pickles with mini poppadoms
- Plate raita with naan bread

Rolled courgette ribbons
with mint, chillies, and goat's cheese

Small courgettes have a sweet, buttery taste and their flesh is tender, making it easier to create ribbons. Secure the rolls with toothpicks rather than chives if you prefer.

1 Heat the grill to high. Using a very sharp knife, cut the courgettes into 20 lengthways slices, about 5mm (¼in) thick. Brush the slices with 2 tablespoons of the olive oil and sprinkle with the salt and pepper. Put them in a grill pan and cook on both sides until the courgettes have grill stripes. Take care not to overcook or they will break apart when rolling. Set aside to cool.

2 Heat the remaining oil in a frying pan, add the chillies, and fry until crisp around the edges. Drain on kitchen towel.

3 Bring a small saucepan of water to the boil, drop in the chives and remove immediately with a slotted spoon. Place in cold water briefly, then leave to dry on kitchen towel. This prevents them breaking during tying.

4 Spread each courgette slice with about 1 teaspoon of goat's cheese. Place a couple of mint leaves, 2–3 chilli slivers, and some rocket across one end so that they protrude. Gently roll the slice up and secure it with a toothpick. Tie a chive around the roll and trim the ends with scissors. Remove the toothpicks and refrigerate until serving.

Prepare ahead
The courgettes can be grilled and the chillies sautéed on the morning of serving, then refrigerated. The rolls can be prepared 2 hours ahead. To prevent them becoming soggy, they should be covered with kitchen towel, then plastic wrap.

INGREDIENTS

4–5 small courgettes

3 tbsp extra virgin olive oil

½ tsp each salt and pepper

2 thumb-sized red chillies, de-seeded and thinly sliced

Small bunch of fresh chives

100g (3½oz) mild goat's cheese

15g (½oz) fresh mint

2 small handfuls of baby rocket, long stems trimmed

Toothpicks, to secure

Preparation time 20 minutes
Cooking time 10–15 minutes
Makes 20 rolls

BUY AND ARRANGE

Avocado with balsamic vinegar (*see p173*) • white bean dip (*see p71*) • brownies with chocolate sauce (*see p214*)

PARTNER WITH

Spinach and yoghurt dip (*see p66*) • cumin lamb skewers (*see p112*) • spinach and peppered pear salad (*see p84*)

Roasted pepper and mozzarella
with warm anchovy agrodulce dressing

If you are short on time, use peppadews instead of roasting the peppers yourself. These sweet and sour pickled baby peppers work fantastically with the mild cheese.

1 Preheat the grill to high. Place the peppers, skin side up, on a non-stick baking tray and cook under the grill for 5 minutes, until blackened. Transfer to a sealed plastic bag for 5 minutes, then remove and peel. Cut into 2.5cm (1in) wide strips and set aside.

2 To make the dressing, place the oil in a small sauté pan, add the garlic and anchovy and gently fry until golden. Add the vinegar, chillies, honey, onion, salt, and pepper, and simmer the mixture for 2–3 minutes, until syrupy.

3 Tear the mozzarella into pieces. Divide the salad ingredients between individual plates or on a platter. Drizzle over the warm dressing and sprinkle with the mint and basil leaves.

Prepare ahead

The peppers can be prepared the day before, and refrigerated. The dressing can be made on the morning of serving and warmed through before using.

INGREDIENTS

6 red peppers, de-seeded and quartered

3 fresh buffalo mozzarella balls, drained

Small handful of fresh basil and mint leaves

Dressing

75ml (2½fl oz) extra virgin olive oil

2 garlic cloves, thinly sliced

1 anchovy, rinsed

75ml (2½fl oz) red wine vinegar

½ tsp crushed red chillies

1½ tsp honey

1 small red onion, thinly sliced

½ tsp each salt and pepper

Preparation time 20 minutes

Cooking time 5 minutes

Makes 8 small plates, 4 starters, or a platter

BUY AND ARRANGE

Crushed feta dip (see p70) • spice-dusted prawns (see p148) • biscotti, mascarpone, and dessert wine (see p215)

PARTNER WITH

Fried artichokes Roman style (see p12) • sage and lemon meatballs (see p131)

Roasted butternut squash
with soy balsamic dressing

Butternut squash becomes sweet and creamy when roasted and shows a surprising affinity with strong Asian ingredients such as soy sauce.

1 Preheat the oven to 200°C (400°F/Gas mark 6). Place the squash on a baking sheet and drizzle with the olive oil, salt, and pepper. Bake for 20 minutes, shaking the tray a few times to avoid any sticking. Remove from the oven and set aside until needed.

2 Place the dressing ingredients in a jar, close the lid, and shake well. Place the rocket on the plates and arrange the squash on top. Pour the dressing over and top with sesame seeds, spring onion, and coriander leaves.

Prepare ahead
The butternut squash and dressing can be made the morning of serving. Under-cook the squash and then reheat before serving. Serve within half an hour of dressing.

INGREDIENTS

1 large butternut squash, peeled, de-seeded, and cut into 2.5cm (1in) cubes

2 tbsp olive oil

1 tsp each sea salt and pepper

4 large handfuls of rocket

1 tsp toasted sesame seeds

4 spring onions, finely sliced

Small handful fresh coriander

Dressing

6 tbsp extra virgin olive oil

3 tbsp balsamic vinegar

1 tbsp soy sauce

1 medium-sized red chilli, de-seeded and finely chopped

½ garlic clove, finely chopped

1 tsp honey

Juice of ½ lime

Preparation time 15 minutes
Cooking time 20 minutes
Makes 8 small salads or 4 starters

BUY AND ARRANGE

Watercress salad with spring onion (*see p93*) • prawn and cucumber skewers (*see p149*) • fresh lychees (*see p215*)

PARTNER WITH

Pork and prawn dumplings (*see p184*) • avocado crostini (*see p164*)

Avocado crostini
with cream cheese and sweet chilli

Although it may seem strange to team avocado with Asian flavours, chilli is actually magnificent when juxtaposed with creamy-flavoured ingredients.

1 Preheat the oven to 200°C (400°F/Gas mark 6). To make the crostini, place the bread slices on a non-stick baking sheet. Brush with 3 tablespoons of oil and season. Bake for 6 minutes, until browned on the edges but chewy in the centre. Rub with the garlic and set the crostini aside.

2 Spread the crostini with 1–2 teaspoons of cream cheese. Top with 2 slices of avocado, then the spring onions. Drizzle with the sweet chilli dipping sauce, sprinkle with the chilli, and serve.

Prepare ahead
The bread slices can be prepared 2 days before, and stored in an airtight container. The crostinis can be assembled half an hour before serving, but squeeze a little lemon or lime juice over the avocado to prevent browning.

INGREDIENTS

16 x 5cm (2in) square slices of sourdough baguette or other chewy bread

3 tbsp olive oil

1 garlic clove, peeled

200g (7oz) cream cheese

4 avocado halves, each cut into 4 slices

4 spring onions, with stems, finely chopped

1 recipe sweet chilli and coriander sauce (*see p218*), or bottled sweet chilli dipping sauce, to drizzle

2 thumb-sized chillies, de-seeded and thinly sliced

Preparation time 10 minutes
Cooking time 6 minutes
Makes 16 crostini

BUY AND ARRANGE

Asian cucumber salad (*see p93*) • spicy peanut dip (*see p71*) • prawn and cucumber skewers (*see p149*)

PARTNER WITH

Red curry pumpkin soup (*see p46*) • glass noodle salad (*see p76*) • coconut macaroons (*see p210*)

Gorgonzola crostini
with seared garlic greens and sultanas

Blanching greens before searing keeps their colour bright and removes any potential bitterness. Any other bread, such as ciabatta, can be used in place of the sourdough.

1 To make the crostini, preheat the oven to 200°C (400°F/Gas mark 6). Place the bread slices on a non-stick baking sheet and brush with 3 tablespoons of the oil. Sprinkle with half of the salt and some black pepper. Bake for 6 minutes, until browned on the edges but still chewy in the centre. Rub the bread with one of the garlic cloves and set aside.

2 Bring some salted water to the boil, add the kale, then reduce the heat and simmer for about 5 minutes or until cooked but firm. Drain and immediately plunge into iced water to preserve the colour and halt the cooking. Drain, pressing out as much water as possible with your hands and set aside.

3 Finely slice the garlic cloves. Heat the remaining oil in a large frying pan. Add the garlic and chillies, and brown lightly. Add the drained kale and toss to combine the flavours. Stir in the sultanas, pine nuts, and vinegar. Toss again to heat through.

4 Spread the gorgonzola thickly over the crostini. Spoon over the kale mixture, garnish with the Parmesan shavings and serve.

Prepare ahead

The crostini can be made 2 days in advance and stored in an airtight container. The greens can be cooked on the morning of serving and refrigerated, but don't toss with the remaining ingredients until 1 hour before serving, to retain the green colour.

INGREDIENTS

16 thin slices sourdough

6 tbsp extra virgin olive oil

1 tsp salt

Freshly ground black pepper

2 garlic cloves, peeled

4 large handfuls or 200g (7oz) curly kale or other greens, chopped into 2.5cm (1in) pieces

½ tsp crushed red chillies

1 tbsp sultanas, soaked in warm water for 10 minutes

2 tbsp pine nuts, toasted

3 tbsp balsamic vinegar

100g (3½oz) gorgonzola

Parmesan shavings, to garnish

Preparation time 15 minutes
Cooking time 12 minutes
Makes 16 crostini

BUY AND ARRANGE

Baby prawns with rocket (*see p149*) • shaved celery salad (*see p92*) • marinated olives with orange (*see p30*)

PARTNER WITH

Mushroom and chestnut soup (*see p38*) • chunky aubergine sticks (*see p23*) • artichoke puff pastry bites (*see p196*)

Baby beetroot and bresaola
with creamy horseradish dressing

The skin of baby beetroot is delicious when roasted, so don't spend time peeling it when making this pretty crimson and green salad.

1 Preheat the oven to 200°C (400°F/Gas mark 6). Place the beetroot on a large piece of heavy foil. Add the thyme sprigs, salt and pepper, and spoon over the olive oil. Fold over the foil to create an airtight packet. Bake for 45 minutes, or until easily pierced with a knife. Unwrap, trim the stems, and cut each beetroot in half. Place in a bowl and sprinkle with the red wine vinegar.

2 Mix the dressing ingredients in a small bowl. Divide the rocket, bresaola, and the halved beetroot between 8 small plates. Just before serving, spoon over the dressing, and sprinkle with chives or parsley.

Prepare ahead
The beetroot can be roasted and the dressing prepared on the morning of serving, then covered and refrigerated. Arrange just before serving.

INGREDIENTS

10–12 baby beetroot or 4 medium-sized beetroot, cut into quarters

2 sprigs of thyme

½ tsp each salt and pepper

3 tbsp extra virgin olive oil

2 tbsp red wine vinegar

Small handful rocket leaves

4 slices bresaola, proscuitto or Serrano ham, torn in half

Chopped fresh chives or parsley, to garnish

Dressing

1 tbsp grated horseradish, bottled or fresh

5 tbsp crème fraîche or sour cream

1 tsp white wine or rice vinegar

1 tbsp of lemon juice

1 tbsp grated lemon zest

½ tsp each salt and pepper

Preparation time 15 minutes
Cooking time 45 minutes
Makes 8 small plates

BUY AND ARRANGE	PARTNER WITH
Tomato and feta skewers (see p31) • marinated anchovies (see p30) • spice-dusted prawns (see p148)	Yellow lentil soup (see p44) • Serrano-wrapped prawns (see p108) • peach and raspberry crisps (see p212)

Grilled baby aubergines
with miso dressing

Miso is a fermented soy bean paste from Japan. Its nutty, salty tones complement the subtlety of aubergines. Use baby aubergines if you can since they have a silky, soft texture.

1 Preheat the oven to 200°C (400°F/Gas mark 6). If using baby aubergines, slice in half lengthways, leaving stems on. For larger aubergines, cut into 2½cm (1in) slices. Cut a criss-cross pattern into the flesh. Drizzle with the oil and season. Transfer to a non-stick baking tray, and bake for about 20 minutes, until golden.

2 In a small bowl, combine the dressing ingredients, mixing well. Spread the mixture thickly on the aubergines and sprinkle with the sesame seeds. Place under the grill for 1–2 minutes. Serve garnished with the spring onion and accompanied by any leftover dressing as a dip.

Prepare ahead
The dressing can be made the night before and the aubergines can be roasted 4 hours before and then grilled just before serving.

INGREDIENTS

12 baby, or 4 small, aubergines

2 tbsp vegetable or olive oil

½ tsp each salt and pepper

1 tsp sesame seeds

4 spring onions, chopped, to garnish

Dressing

85g (3oz) miso paste (preferably light-coloured)

3 tbsp sugar

3 tbsp sake

Juice of ½ lime and ½ lemon

½ tsp chilli flakes, or ½ fresh red chilli, finely chopped

Preparation time 10 minutes
Cooking time 22 minutes
Makes 8 servings

BUY AND ARRANGE

Watercress salad with spring onion (*see p93*) • fresh oysters (*see p148*) • caramelized grilled pineapple (*see p214*)

PARTNER WITH

Roasted butternut squash (*see p162*) • Peking seared duck rolls (*see p180*) • seared sesame tuna (*see p138*)

Quick vegetables
buy and arrange ideas to create simple recipes

Often it is the most simple dishes that work best, especially if you find quality, in-season produce. Vegetable dishes can be a sticking point for many people, so timesaving ideas are the answer by simply roasting or grilling, and seasoning well. Be adventurous and try something new, such as the roasted shallots – so simple yet delicious.

Roasted sweet potato wedges with cumin

Cut 3 large, peeled sweet potatoes into wedges, about 2.5cm (1in) in size, drizzle with 2 tablespoons olive oil and 2 teaspoons whole cumin seeds. Roast them in an oven preheated to 200°C (400°F/Gas mark 6) for 30–40 minutes, until crispy. Shake the baking tray frequently during cooking to prevent sticking. Serve warm.

Piquillo peppers with sherry vinegar

Drain a 200g (7oz) jar of Spanish piquillo peppers or roasted red peppers and thinly slice them. Mix the peppers with 1 teaspoon sherry vinegar, 1 tablespoon extra virgin olive oil, and 1 small handful chopped parsley, then season. Serve with toasted bread.

Roasted asparagus with soy sauce, balsamic vinegar, and walnut oil

Trim 2 bunches of asparagus and toss them with 1 teaspoon soy sauce, 1 tablespoon walnut oil, and 1 tablespoon balsamic vinegar, then season. Roast them in the oven for about 15 minutes at 200°C (400°F/Gas mark 6) until golden. Alternatively, cook them in a grill pan and pour over the vinaigrette after. Serve warm.

Grilled chicory with vinegar

Slice 2–3 small heads of chicory in half lengthways. Brush each half with 1 teaspoon olive oil, then season. Put the chicory in a grill pan with the cut-side facing downwards and grill them until golden. Splash each half with some sherry or balsamic vinegar after cooking. Place them on a serving dish to be picked up and eaten by hand.

Roasted peppers with garlic

Cut 3 red peppers in half and remove the seeds. Fill each half with a few halved cherry tomatoes, 2 slices of a garlic clove, 3 capers, and 2–3 basil leaves, then season. Bake at 200°C (400°F/Gas mark 6) for 30–40 minutes, until golden. Rip 2 fresh mozzarella balls into pieces. Top the pepper halves with the mozzarella while they are still warm so that the cheese melts, then serve.

Marinated Italian mushrooms

In a bowl, toss 500g (1lb) small white button mushrooms with 3 tablespoons extra virgin olive oil, 2 tablespoons balsamic vinegar, 1 teaspoon crushed fennel seeds, a pinch of crushed chillis, and 1 teaspoon honey, then season. Let sit for 30 minutes to marinate, then serve.

Steamed edamame with sea salt

Steam 500g (1lb) frozen edamame soybeans until heated through and slightly softened, but still holding their shape, about 4 minutes. Serve them in a dish sprinkled with 1 tablespoon soy sauce and 1 teaspoon flaked sea salt. Edamame can be found in speciality food shops or bought online (*see p223*).

Carrots in vinaigrette

Peel and cut 4 large carrots into slices, blanche them in boiling water until al dente, then place in a dish. In a bowl, mix together 3 tablespoons red wine vinegar, 5 tablespoons extra virgin olive oil, 1 chopped garlic clove, and 1 small handful chopped parsley. Pour the mixture over the warm carrots and marinate in a refrigerator as it cools for at least 1 hour or preferably overnight.

Avocado with balsamic vinegar and dill

Cut 3–4 avocados in half, remove the stone, and rub with a little lemon juice. Into each half add 1 teaspoon extra virgin olive oil, 1 teaspoon balsamic vinegar, and 1 small handful freshly chopped dill, then season. Serve immediately.

Roasted shallots

In a baking tray, toss 15 small to medium-sized unpeeled shallots with 1 tablespoon olive oil, and roast for 30 minutes at 200°C (400°F/Gas mark 6). Serve warm and allow guests to peel them as they eat.

Roasted new potatoes with smoky paprika

Roasted new potatoes with smoky paprika

In a bowl, toss 500g (1lb) small new potatoes with 2 tablespoons olive oil and 1 teaspoon either smoky paprika, pimenton, or chilli powder. Roast them for 30 minutes in an oven preheated to 200°C (400°F/Gas mark 6). Serve them with a dip and toothpicks to pick them up.

Radishes with tapenade and chilled butter

Trim the bottoms off 3–4 handfuls of radishes, but leave the tops untrimmed to be used as handles. Serve them with a good-quality black olive tapenade and some chilled butter to dip.

Each small parcel that you prepare is a present with a succulent treasure waiting inside. First, select your favourite wrapper from the vast selection available, such as tortillas, rice papers, and pastries. Then create a piquant filling of vegetables, seafood, or cheese, and get rolling.

Wrapped, tied, and rolled

Seafood spring rolls
with sweet chilli and coriander sauce

Take a bite of one of these Vietnamese specialties and you will be overwhelmed by an intense aroma of fresh herbs. Unlike fried rolls, these wrappers are made of rice paper.

1 Arrange the seafood, onion, carrots, ginger, and herbs in separate piles on a tray. Place a large clean tea towel on a work surface, and fill a medium-sized bowl with hot water.

2 Drop one rice paper wrapper at a time into the hot water for about 30 seconds. When soft and pliable, place the wrapper on the tea towel and dab off excess water with another towel. Fill the lower side of the wrapper with 1 tablespoon of seafood, and lay some onion, carrot, and herbs across the other side, allowing them to protrude from the top of the wrapper. Fold up the lower, front side, then fold in the side and roll up to make a tight parcel. Repeat with the remaining wrappers. Serve with sticky chilli jam.

Prepare ahead

The rolls may be made the night before, covered with 2 pieces of kitchen towel and then in plastic wrap, and stored in the refrigerator.

INGREDIENTS

250g (8oz) mixed cooked seafood, such as white crab meat, peeled prawns, and lobster meat

1 red onion, thinly sliced

2 large carrots, very thinly sliced

5cm (2in) root ginger, very thinly sliced

20 coriander sprigs, about 7½cm (3in) long

40 fresh mint leaves

20 x 15cm (6in) wide circular rice paper wrappers

1 recipe sweet chilli and coriander sauce (*see p218*) or bottled sweet chilli dipping sauce, to serve

Preparation time 1 hour
Makes 20 rolls

BUY AND ARRANGE

Prawn and cucumber skewers (*see p149*) • watercress salad with spring onion (*see p93*) • sliced watermelon (*see p215*)

PARTNER WITH

Thai sweetcorn fritters (*see p26*) • lemongrass beef skewers (*see p104*) • seared duck and mango salad (*see p90*)

Soft shell steak tacos
with smoky tomatillo sauce

Tomatillos look like little green tomatoes covered in sticky paper. If fresh ones are not available, use canned: 300g (11oz) canned tomatillos are equivalent to 500g (1lb) fresh.

1 In a large bowl, mix together the olive oil, chilli powder, salt, and pepper. Add the meat, turn to coat, and marinate for 30 minutes.

2 To make the sauce, soak the onions in the lime juice. Meanwhile, pan-fry the garlic for 8 minutes in a dry non-stick frying pan over moderate heat. Stir until soft and blackened. Leave to cool, then peel. Place the tomatillos on a baking sheet and cook under a high grill for 8 minutes, until blackened. Leave to cool.

3 Place the garlic, tomatillos, chipotles, coriander, salt, and pepper into a food processor or blender. Purée coarsely. Fold in the onion mixture and set aside

4 Heat the grill to medium. Remove the meat from marinade and grill for 3 minutes on each side, or until medium rare. Cover with foil, leave to rest for 10 minutes, then slice thinly across the grain. Toss the spring onions in a little oil, season, and grill briefly. Fill the tacos with the steak slices, smoky tomatillo sauce, crème fraîche, carrot escabeche, if using, onions, and lettuce. Serve immediately. Alternatively, allow the guests to make their own tacos.

Prepare ahead

The steaks can be marinated for up to 2 days in the refrigerator. The sauce can be made the day before and refrigerated.

INGREDIENTS

1 tbsp olive oil

½ tsp smoky chilli powder

½ tsp each salt and pepper

2 x 250g (8oz) sirloin, rump, or fillet steaks

8 spring onions

Olive oil, for grilling

16 ready-made taco shells

200g (7oz) crème fraîche or sour cream

1 recipe carrot escabeche, optional (see p216)

16 baby lettuce leaves, to serve

Sauce

1 small red onion, finely diced

Juice of 1 lime

8 large garlic cloves, unpeeled

1kg (2lb) tomatillos, husked and rinsed

2 chipotles in adobo

Small bunch fresh coriander

½ tsp each salt and pepper

Preparation time 15 minutes, plus 30 minutes marinating
Cooking time 30 minutes
Makes 16 small tacos

BUY AND ARRANGE	PARTNER WITH
Palm heart and avocado salad (see p92) • fruit salsa (see p70) • padron peppers (see p30)	Serrano-wrapped prawns (see p108) • crab and gruyére nachos (see p142)

Peking seared duck rolls
with plum sauce

This twist on a classic calls for authentic Chinese pancakes, but small tortillas work nicely, too. Be sure to heat them for a few seconds so that they roll without cracking.

1 In a medium-sized bowl, combine the soy sauce, honey, and ginger. Score the outside of the duck in a criss-cross pattern and add it to the soy mixture. Sprinkle with black pepper, turn to coat, and leave to marinate for at least 1 hour.

2 Remove the duck from the marinade and dry on kitchen towel. Heat a non-stick frying pan and add the duck, skin side down. Cook very slowly over a low heat for about 10 minutes, pouring the duck fat off as it melts to prevent spattering. When the skin is thin and crispy, turn the duck, and cook on the other side for another 5 minutes. Leave to rest for 10 minutes, then slice very thinly into about 10 slices per breast.

3 Spread each pancake with 1 teaspoon of the sauce, then place 1 slice of duck, a couple of chives, and some spring onion and cucumber on top. Roll up the pancake and tie it with an additional chive, or secure it with a chopstick, so that it stays closed.

Prepare ahead

The duck can be left to marinate, covered, in the refrigerator for 2 days, cooked the day before and again refrigerated. The onions can be sliced 2 hours ahead. The rolls can be assembled 2 hours before serving and covered with kitchen paper then plastic wrap.

INGREDIENTS

2 tbsp soy sauce

1 tbsp honey

1 tbsp ground ginger

2 duck breasts

Ground black pepper

20 Peking pancakes

1 jar Chinese plum or hoisin sauce

Small handful of chives

4 spring onions, cut into matchsticks

1 medium cucumber, cut into thin matchsticks

Preparation time 10 minutes, plus 1 hour marinating time

Cooking time 15 minutes

Makes 20 small rolls

BUY AND ARRANGE

Crab and cream cheese dip (see p71) • spice-dusted prawns (see p148) • caramelized grilled pineapple (see p215)

PARTNER WITH

Thai sweetcorn fritters (see p26) • Hainanese chicken (see p127) • roasted butternut squash (see p163)

Saffron feta filo triangles
with preserved lemon and onion

Preserved lemons, a Moroccan speciality, add salty sharpness without the bitterness of fresh lemon rind. It is easy to cure a jar of them at home, or they can be found in specialist shops or bought on-line (*see p223*).

1 Put the oil in a medium-sized sauté pan, add the onion and season. Sauté for about 8 minutes, until the onion is soft.

2 Add the garlic, preserved lemon, pimenton, and saffron, and cook for a further 2–3 minutes. Transfer the mixture to a bowl and leave to cool. When cold, add the crumbled feta cheese and mix gently. Season to taste.

3 Preheat the oven to 200°C (400°F/Gas mark 6). Place a baking sheet in the oven. Carefully lift 1 sheet of filo pastry and cut it in half lengthways, to make a long strip of pastry. Keep the remaining pastry covered with a tea towel while you work, to prevent it from drying out. Brush the pastry strip with melted butter. Place a tablespoon of the filling at one end and fold the pastry over from one corner to enclose the filling and form a triangle. Continue folding, alternating from side to side, until the filling is well-wrapped, then cut the pastry. Brush with more melted butter. Repeat with the remaining pastry, and place in the refrigerator until you are ready to cook.

4 Carefully transfer the triangles to the preheated baking tray and bake for 15 minutes, until golden brown. Serve warm with Greek yoghurt or sweet tomato jam.

Prepare ahead
The triangles can be prepared the day before, covered with plastic wrap, then kitchen paper, and refrigerated until ready to cook.

INGREDIENTS

4 tbsp olive oil

1 large onion, finely chopped

3 garlic cloves, finely chopped

½ preserved lemon, skin only, rinsed well and finely chopped

½ tsp pimenton

½ tsp saffron threads, crushed and soaked in 1 tbsp hot water

200g (7oz) feta cheese, crumbled

270g (9oz) filo pastry

Melted butter or oil, for brushing

Greek yoghurt or sweet tomato jam (*see p218*), to serve

Preparation time 30 minutes
Cooking time 25 minutes
Makes 20 triangles

BUY AND ARRANGE

Baby lettuce with sherry vinegar and walnut oil (*see p92*) • houmous with smoked paprika (*see p70*) • oranges with rose water (*see p214*)

PARTNER WITH

Spinach and yoghurt dip (*see p66*) • yellow lentil soup (*see p44*) • cardamom-poached apricots (*see p211*)

Pork and prawn dumplings
with garlic oil

These dumplings are easier to make than you might think, so give them a try. Both gyoza and wonton wrappers can be found at Asian supermarkets and they freeze well.

1 To make the filling, place the 2 whole garlic cloves, ginger, and coriander in a food processor, and process well. Add the onions, water chestnuts, ginger, prawns, pork, cornflour, egg white, and soy sauce, and process again to mix.

2 Hold a wrapper in your hand and spoon in 1 tablespoon of the filling. Fold the wrapper around to enclose the filling, pleating it, but keeping the top open. Press down slightly to flatten the bottom then place on a plastic tray dusted with cornflour. Repeat with the remaining wrappers, then refrigerate until ready to steam. Keep the unused wrappers covered with a tea towel to prevent them from drying out.

3 Heat the oil in a small saucepan, add the chopped garlic, and fry for 1 minute, until golden but not too brown. Remove from the heat and set aside.

4 Fill a saucepan with water to a depth of 5cm (2in) and bring to a boil. Place some parchment paper in the bottom of a bamboo steamer. Arrange 10 dumplings in the steamer so that they are not touching. Cover and steam for 6–8 minutes. Remove and place on a serving dish. Drizzle with the garlic oil, and serve with the ketchup manis. Repeat with the next batch.

Prepare ahead

The dumplings can be made 4 hours in advance and stored in the refrigerator. The uncooked dumplings may be frozen individually on trays, then placed in freezer bags. Thaw in the refrigerator before steaming.

INGREDIENTS

200g (7oz) lean minced pork

200g (7oz) raw peeled prawns

Small bunch fresh coriander

2 spring onions, finely chopped

7 water chestnuts, finely chopped

1cm (½in) root ginger

4 garlic cloves, 2 finely chopped

1 tsp cornflour, plus extra for dusting

1 tsp egg white

1 tsp soy sauce

20 wonton wrappers, cut into circles, or round gyoza wrappers

3 tbsp groundnut or pure vegetable oil

Ketchup manis or soy sauce, to serve

Preparation time 30 minutes
Cooking time 25 minutes
Makes 20 dumplings

BUY AND ARRANGE

Steamed edamame (*see p173*) • Asian cucumber salad (*see p93*) • selection of sushi (*see p30*)

PARTNER WITH

Pork satay (*see p109*) • seared sesame tuna (*see p138*) • passionfruit trifle (*see p206*)

Crispy chorizo quesadillas
with guacamole

The creamy avocado is scrumptious against the melted cheese of these quesadillas. Try making these with different fillings too, such as grilled mushrooms with goat's cheese.

1 Preheat the oven to 140°C (275°F/Gas mark 1). To make the guacamole, mash the avocado in a bowl, using a potato masher. Stir in the garlic, jalapeño, lime juice, Tabasco, and Worcestershire sauce. Mix well and season to taste.

2 To make the quesadillas, place 3 tortillas on the worktop and spread with the cheese, chipotle, chorizo or salami, coriander, and onion. Top each with another tortilla.

3 Heat a large, non-stick frying pan and add 1 tablespoon of the oil. Place one of the quesadillas in the pan and cook over a low to medium heat for 2–3 minutes. When the cheese is beginning to melt, gently turn using a large spatula and cook for a further 2–3 minutes. Keep it warm in the oven while you repeat the process with the remaining quesadillas. Cut each one into 8 pieces and serve with the guacamole.

Prepare ahead

The guacamole can be made the morning of serving, covered with plastic wrap, and refrigerated. The quesadillas can be made 30 minutes before serving and kept warm in an oven preheated to 140°C (275°F/Gas mark 1).

INGREDIENTS

6 large flour tortillas

350g (12oz) Gruyère, Cheddar or other hard, melting cheese, grated

2 chipotles in adobo, de-seeded and chopped

18 thin slices of chorizo or salami

Small handful chopped fresh coriander

3 spring onions, thinly sliced

3 tbsp vegetable oil

Guacamole

Flesh of 3 large, ripe avocados

1 garlic clove, crushed

1 jalapeño pepper, very finely chopped

Juice of 2 limes

1 tsp Tabasco sauce, such as the smoky chipotle variety

1 tbsp Worcestershire sauce

Preparation time 30 minutes
Cooking time 15 minutes
Makes 24 pieces

BUY AND ARRANGE	PARTNER WITH
Palm heart and avocado salad (see p92) • roasted new potatoes with smoky paprika (see p173) • Spanish deli plate (see p30)	Chilli gazpacho (see p36) • salmon and pineapple skewers (see p110) • baby clams (see p136) • mini peach and raspberry crisps (see p212)

Bresaola and pear rolls
with rocket and Parmesan

Bresaola is an Italian dry-cured beef fillet produced in a similar way to prosciutto. Real artisan balsamic vinegar - thick, syrupy, and undeniably expensive - is required here.

1 In a medium-sized bowl, toss the pears in the lemon juice, salt, and pepper.

2 Place 1 pear slice and a few sprigs of rocket on 1 slice of bresaola or prosciutto. Top with a little Parmesan, drizzle with balsamic vinegar, and roll it up. The bresaola will adhere to itself. Cut the roll in half for smaller bites, if you wish. Repeat with the remaining rolls and place seam side down on a serving plate.

Prepare ahead

The rolls can be made 4 hours before serving. Cover with baking parchment or greaseproof paper, then in plastic wrap, and store in the refrigerator.

INGREDIENTS

1 ripe but firm pear, cored, halved and thinly sliced

1 tsp lemon juice

½ tsp each salt and pepper

2 large handfuls of rocket

20 small slices bresaola or 10 slices prosciutto, cut in half

30g (1oz) Parmesan, shaved

2 tbsp good-quality balsamic vinegar

Preparation time 20 minutes
Makes 20 rolls

BUY AND ARRANGE

Chicory salad (*see p93*) • fresh crab crostini (*see p148*) • Parmesan crisps (*see p31*)

PARTNER WITH

Fried artichokes Roman style (*see p12*) • spiced goat's cheese balls (*see p59*) • farro salad (*see p78*)

Colours

- Charcoal black
- Brilliant white
- Berry red
- Chocolate brown
- Oatmeal tan

Tableware

- Bamboo placemats
- Selection of chopsticks
- Square plates
- Small dipping bowls
- Crackle-glazed china

Japanese style

There is a simplicity and purity to Japanese food that sets it apart from other cuisines. Its genius lies in using fresh, quality ingredients rather than a reliance on complicated preparation. Yes, this is an amazingly healthy way to eat, but that's a bonus – the real story is flavour. The clean taste of this cuisine is accented with miso, sesame seeds, and ginger, but it is soy sauce that is at the heart of it all, lending a characteristic of saltiness and depth.

Fresh fish will certainly make an appearance on this menu since it a staple of the Japanese diet. This does not automatically mean sushi since marinated, grilled, fried, and roasted fish dishes also play a big part.

Taste is rivalled by the beauty of presentation too. A Japanese theme means creating a smart table setting that showcases minimalistic perfection. Think dark, sophisticated colours, such as deep reds and black. Plates and bowls have clean lines and smooth textures. Lay out your chopsticks, square plates, and dipping bowls, and let the food shine. Start the evening by sipping a sophisticated cucumber martini and finish with a relaxing green tea.

Flavours

- Fresh ginger
- Salty soy sauce
- Refreshing cucumber
- Sesame seeds
- Sweet or salty miso

Nibbles

- Rice-coated peanuts (*see p31*)
- Unpeeled fresh lychees (*see p215*)
- Selection of sushi (*see p31*)
- Prawn and cucumber skewers (*see p149*)
- Miso halibut bites (*see p140*)

Menu

Crispy scallops
with wasabi mayonnaise

Sticky chicken wings
in teriyaki sauce

Roasted baby aubergines
with miso dressing

Roasted butternut squash
with soy balsamic dressing

Seared sesame tuna
with sweet soy and chilli dressing

Coconut macaroons
dipped in dark chocolate

BUY AND ARRANGE
Prawn and cucumber skewers
(see p149)

Unpeeled fresh lychees
(see p215)

Rice-coated peanuts
(see p31)

Crispy scallops
(see p24)

Sticky chicken wings
(see p126)

Grilled baby aubergines
(see p170)

Roasted butternut squash
(see p163)

Seared sesame tuna
(see p138)

Coconut macaroons
(see p210)

Two days before
- Marinate chicken wings
- Make coconut macaroons

The night before
- Make miso dressing for baby
  aubergines
- Sear, wrap, and refrigerate
  sesame tuna

In the morning
- Bread scallops and make
  wasabi mayonnaise and ponzu
  dipping sauce
- Par-cook roast butternut
  squash and make soy dressing
- Make dressing and chop onion
  and apple for sesame tuna
- Make prawn skewers

Cucumber martini

Ideally, you need a cocktail shaker to make this refreshing tipple. A good-quality shaker is a worthwhile investment.

INGREDIENTS

20 slices of cucumber

Large bunch of mint, stems removed

40ml (1fl oz) sugar syrup

Ice

40ml (1fl oz) dry vermouth

280ml (9fl oz) gin

12 cucumber cubes, batons, or ribbons on toothpicks, to garnish

Toothpicks

Makes 4 martinis,

Chill four martini glasses in the refrigerator. Place the cucumber, mint, and sugar syrup in a cocktail shaker. Shake, then add a handful of ice, the vermouth, and gin. Shake again, then sieve the liquid into the glasses. Garnish with cucumber cubes.

One to two hours before
- Bake chicken wings; keep warm in a low oven under foil
- Roast aubergines and coat with miso dressing
- Slice seared sesame tuna; plate with onion and apple, omit dressing
- Plate lychees

At the last minute
- Plate scallops with sauces
- Plate chicken wings
- Add dressing to sesame tuna
- Plate coconut macaroons
- Make cucumber martinis and pour

Half an hour before
- Prepare martini ingredients and cucumber skewer garnish
- Fry scallops; keep warm in a low oven
- Grill aubergines; plate
- Finish cooking squash; plate
- Plate prawn skewers with a bowl of sweet soy

Pea and prawn samosas
with mango chutney

Amchoor is dried ground mango and can be found in specialist and Indian food stores or can be bought on-line (*see p223*). If you can't find it, use lemon juice instead.

1 Peel the potato and cut it into chunks. Place the potato chunks in a saucepan of boiling, salted water and cook for 10 minutes, or until soft. Mash roughly.

2 Meanwhile, heat the 2 tablespoons of vegetable oil in a frying pan, and add the onion, garlic, and ginger, then season. Sauté for about 8 minutes, until soft. Add the garam masala, cumin seeds, and amchoor. Cook for a few minutes more, then add the potato, peas, and coriander, mixing well. Remove from the heat and transfer to a small bowl. Stir in the raw prawns.

3 Take the wrappers and place 2 tablespoons of the filling in each. Brush the edges with egg white and fold over to seal. If using spring roll wrappers, you will need to place the filling at one corner of the wrapper, then brush all the edges with egg white, and fold in from the filled corner.

4 Put the oil in a heavy-based, medium-sized saucepan. Heat until a small piece of bread, when dropped in, sizzles immediately. Fry 3–4 samosas for about 4 minutes, until crispy. Repeat with the other samosas. Drain on kitchen towel. Serve with the mango chutney and garnish with some coriander sprigs.

Prepare ahead

The samosas can be made and refrigerated the night before. Alternatively, they can be placed in a single layer in an airtight container and frozen for 1 month. Thaw in the refrigerator before frying.

INGREDIENTS

1 large potato, about 250g (8oz)

2 tbsp vegetable oil

1 small onion, finely chopped

1 garlic clove, chopped

1 tbsp root ginger, grated

1½ tsp each garam masala, cumin seeds, and amchoor

150g (5oz) fresh or frozen peas

Small handful of fresh coriander, chopped, plus sprigs to garnish

8 large prawns, roughly chopped

20 gyoza or large spring roll wrappers

1 egg white, lightly beaten

600ml (1 pint) vegetable or peanut oil, for deep-frying

Bottled mango chutney, to serve

Preparation time 20 minutes
Cooking time 20 minutes
Makes 30 small samosas

BUY AND ARRANGE

Raita with naan bread (*see p71*) • Indian sugar-coated fennel seeds (*see p215*)

PARTNER WITH

Tomato and ginger soup (*see p50*) • tandoori chicken thighs (*see p130*)

Artichoke puff pastry bites
with mascarpone and caramelized garlic

Preheating your baking sheet ensures that the base of the pastry crisps up well. If you are short on time, substitute the caramelized garlic for 1 teaspoon of chopped raw garlic.

1 To caramelize the garlic, place the cloves in a small saucepan, cover with water, and boil for 3 minutes. Drain, peel, and slice each clove into 3 pieces.

2 Heat the olive oil in a saucepan over a low heat, add the garlic and colour lightly. Drain off the oil, add the vinegar, rosemary, salt, pepper, and sugar, and cook for 3 minutes, until the liquid is reduced to a thick syrup. Pour onto a plate and leave to cool.

3 Preheat the oven to 200°C (400°F/Gas mark 6) and place a large baking sheet in the oven. In a bowl, combine the mascarpone, Parmesan, prosciutto, lemon, basil, and caramelized garlic.

4 Roll out the pastry to 1cm (½in) thick and cut into 20 squares measuring 7.5cm (3in) on each side. Place a large spoonful of the cheese mixture on one side of each square and top with an artichoke half. Fold over the pastry top to enclose. Press the edges together with a fork, dampening the edges first to ensure that the parcels are sealed.

5 Transfer to the hot baking sheet and bake for about 15 minutes, until golden. Serve immediately.

Prepare ahead
The pastries can be made the night before. Cover with parchment or greaseproof paper, wrap in plastic wrap, and store in the refrigerator until ready to cook.

INGREDIENTS

1 small head of garlic, unpeeled

3 tbsp olive oil

2 tbsp white wine vinegar

1 tsp finely chopped rosemary

Pinch each of salt, pepper, and sugar

100g (3½oz) mascarpone

5 tbsp grated Parmesan

4 slices prosciutto, roughly chopped

Juice of ½ lemon

Small handful basil, chopped

750g (26oz) ready-rolled puff pastry

150g (5 oz) marinated artichokes, drained and cut into halves

Preparation time 40 minutes
Cooking time 15 minutes
Makes 20 bites

BUY AND ARRANGE

Radishes with tapenade (see p173) • gorgonzola crostini (see p31) • chocolate mint ice cream sandwiches (see p215)

PARTNER WITH

Roasted prawns and tomatoes (see p145) • three tomato salad (see p86) • orange and beetroot soup (see p40)

When choosing which pudding, cake, or biscuit to make, please cast aside thoughts of calorie-counting or dieting. Instead, indulge your sweetest cravings. Be extravagant with rich creams, decadent chocolate, sugary frosting, and lustrous, ripe fruit.

Sweets

Chocolate Frangelico pudding
with hazelnuts

Frangelico is an Italian hazelnut liqueur, and it complements this lush dessert very well. Experiment with sweet wines too, but keep servings small as this is an intense indulgence.

1 In a large metal or glass bowl, beat the egg yolks and sugar with a whisk until very fluffy. Place the bowl over a saucepan filled with simmering water and whisk over a low heat for about 5 minutes, until very thick. Whisk in the vanilla, cocoa, mascarpone, and Frangelico. Continue whisking for a 2 further minutes until thick again. Remove from the heat.

2 Pour the mixture into small tea or large espresso cups and refrigerate for 4 hours to set. Spoon some whipped cream on each, sprinkle with the chopped nuts, and serve.

Prepare ahead

The puddings can be made the night before and refrigerated.

INGREDIENTS

4 egg yolks

100g (3½oz) caster sugar

½ tsp vanilla extract

4 tbsp good-quality cocoa powder

250g (8oz) mascarpone

60ml (2fl oz) Frangelico or sweet wine

175ml (6fl oz) double cream, whipped

45g (1½oz) toasted and chopped hazelnuts

Preparation time 30 minutes, plus 4 hours refrigerating time

Serves 8 small cups

BUY AND ARRANGE

Shaved celery salad (*see p92*) • yoghurt and dill dip (*see p71*) • spice-dusted prawns (*see p148*)

PARTNER WITH

Baby beetroot and bresaola (*see p168*) • roasted prawns and tomatoes (*see p145*) • mushroom and chestnut soup (*see p38*)

Chocolate cupcakes
with buttercream frosting

These cupcakes deserve a liberal topping of frosting. The decorations, such as rose petals, don't have to be sedate and grown-up - playfulness is the point.

1   To make the cupcakes, preheat the oven to 180°C (350°F/Gas mark 4). Line a 5cm (2in) deep muffin tin with the cupcake cases and set aside. In a bowl, combine the flour and bicarbonate of soda. Put the chocolate in a second bowl and place over a saucepan of simmering water. Stir until melted and smooth.

2   Using a food processor or hand mixer, cream the butter and both sugars until smooth. Beat in the eggs one at a time, then beat in the melted chocolate. Add the sour cream or crème fraîche, vanilla, and flour mixture, and continue beating until smooth. Spoon the batter into the cases until three quarters full. Bake for 20 minutes. Leave to cool in the tin, then transfer to a wire rack.

3   Meanwhile, to make the frosting place the butter in a food processor or mixer. Beat until smooth, then beat in the sugar. Work in the milk, food colouring, and vanilla, adding more milk, if necessary, to achieve a thick but creamy consistency. Spread the cakes liberally with the frosting, top with the rose petals, and serve.

Prepare ahead

The cakes can be made the day before and stored in an airtight container. Spread with the frosting on the day of serving.

INGREDIENTS

10 paper cupcake cases

125g (4oz) plain flour

1 tsp bicarbonate of soda

100g (3½oz) plain baking chocolate, broken into pieces

125g (4oz) unsalted butter, softened

100g (3½oz) caster sugar

100g (3½oz) soft brown sugar

2 large eggs

60g (2oz) sour cream or crème fraîche

1 tsp vanilla extract

Rose petals, to decorate

Frosting

125g (4oz) unsalted butter

350g (12oz) icing sugar

2 tbsp full-fat milk

½ tsp pink food colouring

1 tsp vanilla extract

Preparation time 20 minutes
Cooking time 20 minutes
Makes 10 cupcakes

BUY AND ARRANGE	PARTNER WITH
Crushed feta dip (see p70) • watermelon and feta salad (see p93) • tuna tartare on cucumber slices (see p148)	Seared beef carpaccio (see p128) • chickpea and chilli dip (see p68) • citrus swordfish brochettes (see p96)

Chocolate crinkle cookies
with walnuts

These densely rich chocolate cookies are rolled in icing sugar before baking, a trick that gives a snowy finish and a dramatic contrast in colour.

1 Place the chocolate and butter in a bowl over a saucepan of simmering water, and stir with a spatula until melted and smooth. Remove from heat and set aside to cool slightly.

2 In a medium-sized bowl, combine the flour, baking powder, and salt. In a large bowl, beat together the eggs and sugar with an electric or hand-held whisk for about 2 minutes, until pale. Reduce the speed and whisk in the melted chocolate and the vanilla. Add the flour mixture and continue to whisk until combined, then stir in the walnuts. Cover the bowl and refrigerate for at least 1½ hours.

3 Preheat the oven to 160°C (325°F/Gas mark 3). Line one large or two smaller baking sheets with baking parchment. Place the icing sugar in a bowl. Shape the dough into 3–4cm (1–1½in) balls and roll in the sugar. Transfer to a baking sheet and push down slightly with your hand. Bake for 12–15 minutes, until the edges are set but the centres are still soft. Leave to cool on the baking sheet for 5 minutes, then transfer to a wire rack to cool completely.

Prepare ahead

The dough can be prepared 2 days ahead, covered, and refrigerated until ready to bake. Alternatively, the baked cookies may be stored in an airtight container for 5 days.

INGREDIENTS

175g (6oz) plain chocolate, chopped

60g (2oz) unsalted butter

175g (6oz) plain flour

¾ tsp baking powder

Pinch of salt

2 large eggs, at room temperature

150g (5oz) sugar

1 tsp vanilla extract

125g (4oz) walnuts, roughly chopped

60g (2oz) icing sugar

Preparation time 20 minutes, plus 1½ hours refrigeration time
Cooking time 15 minutes
Makes 20–25 cookies

BUY AND ARRANGE

Parmesan crisps (see p31) • gorgonzola crostini (see p31) • crushed feta dip (see p70)

PARTNER WITH

Sicilian artichoke bottoms (see p154) • chunky aubergine sticks (see p23) • baby clams (see p136)

Passion fruit trifle
with strawberries and mascarpone

Trifles are a simple way to showcase colourful, seasonal fruit. Feel free to substitute your favourites, using the same quantities given in this recipe.

1 Beat the mascarpone, egg yolks, vanilla, and sugar in a bowl until smooth. In a separate bowl, whisk the double cream until thick but still soft. Fold the mascarpone into the cream and set aside.

2 Cut the passion fruit in half and scoop the pulp into a small bowl. Remove the crust from the brioche, if using. Break up the brioche or cake into smaller pieces.

3 Layer the ingredients into glasses, starting with the brioche, then some passion fruit pulp, strawberries, and a drizzle of Marsala, and finishing with a dollop of the mascarpone cream. Top the trifles with the remaining fruit. Refrigerate until serving.

Prepare ahead

The trifles can be assembled the night before, and refrigerated.

INGREDIENTS

250g (8oz) mascarpone

2 egg yolks

1 tsp vanilla extract

60g (2oz) castor sugar

280ml (10fl oz) double cream

8 passion fruit

150g (5oz) brioche or plain sponge cake

250g (8oz) strawberries, stems removed and sliced

125ml (4fl oz) Marsala or other liqueur

Preparation time 20 minutes

Makes 8 small servings

BUY AND ARRANGE

Pan-fried chorizo (see p149) • tomato and feta skewers (see p31) • roasted garlic with warm bread (see p71)

PARTNER WITH

Bagna cauda dip (see p54) • Ithaca courgette cakes (see p28) • seared beef carpaccio (see p128)

Strawberries and figs
dipped in chocolate and hazelnuts

Inexpensive baking chocolate with a low cocoa butterfat content is best here because it doesn't become grainy as it melts. Try using white chocolate too, or a mixture of both.

1 Break the chocolate into pieces, place in a bowl, and heat over a pan of simmering water for about 5 minutes, until melted. Stir occasionally, until smooth. Alternatively, you can melt it in a glass bowl in the microwave for 2 minutes.

2 Cover a large plate with plastic wrap. Dip the fruit into the melted chocolate so it reaches halfway up. Dip into the chopped nuts. Spread out on the plate and keep refrigerated until ready to serve.

Prepare ahead

These can be made on the morning of serving, covered in parchment paper, then plastic wrap, and refrigerated.

INGREDIENTS

200g (7oz) plain baking chocolate

250g (½lb) medium strawberries with hulls left

2 figs, cut into quarters

100g (3½oz) pistachios or toasted hazelnuts, finely chopped

Preparation time 10 minutes

Makes 2 servings

BUY AND ARRANGE

Parmesan crisps (*see p31*) • houmous with smoked paprika (*see p70*) • chicory salad (*see p93*)

PARTNER WITH

Halloumi and sourdough spiedini (*see p106*) • chunky aubergine sticks (*see p23*) • bresaola and pear rolls (*see p188*)

Raspberry meringues
with white chocolate swirls

Follow these golden rules for perfect meringues: use a clean, grease-free mixing bowl for maximum volume, use room-temperature egg whites, and beat them to a stiff gloss.

1   Preheat the oven to 180°C (350°F/Gas mark 4). Line a baking tray with baking parchment. Place the egg whites in a very clean mixing bowl with the salt. Using a balloon whisk, whisk the whites until they are stiff. Slowly whisk in the sugar, 1 tablespoon at a time. At this point the mixture should be glossy and very stiff. Add the vinegar and cornflour and mix again.

2   Place the white chocolate in a glass bowl over a saucepan of simmering water and stir until completely melted.

3   Spoon the meringue mixture onto the baking tray to make 8 large meringues. Take about 4 raspberries and a heaped teaspoon of the melted chocolate and swirl through each meringue, taking care not to flatten it. Ensure that the chocolate is well incorporated: if too exposed, it may brown during cooking.

4   Bake in the oven for 5 minutes, then reduce the heat to 140°C (275°F/Gas mark 1) for 45 minutes. Leave to cool to room temperature, then transfer to a wire rack. Top with spoonfuls of whipped cream, the reserved raspberries, and some pistachios.

Prepare ahead

The meringues can be made the night before and stored in an airtight container, layered between sheets of baking parchment or greaseproof paper. Assemble up to half an hour before serving.

Variations

Try other flavours such as chocolate with flaked almonds, banana with caramel sauce, or coconut with mango and blueberries.

INGREDIENTS

5 organic egg whites

Pinch of salt

275g (10oz) caster sugar

2 tsp cornflour

1 tsp vinegar

75g (2½oz) white chocolate buttons or other inexpensive white chocolate, broken into pieces

150g (5oz) raspberries

250ml (8fl oz) double cream, whipped

10g pistachios, chopped

Preparation time 20 minutes
Cooking time 50 minutes
Makes 8 large or 16 small

BUY AND ARRANGE

Fresh fig, prosciutto, and mozzarella salad (see p92)
• Italian deli plate (see p30)
• spice-dusted prawns (see p148)

PARTNER WITH

Cumin lamb skewers (see p112) • orange and beetroot soup (see p40) • spiced goat's cheese balls (see p59)

Coconut macaroons
dipped in dark chocolate

This delicate confection is just right for Mediterranean or Asian meus and is equally as good without the chocolate.

1 Preheat the oven to 150°C (300°F/Gas mark 2). Line a large baking sheet with baking parchment. Whisk the egg whites until they are thick and form soft peaks. Slowly whisk in the sugar, a quarter at a time, and the vanilla. Fold in the coconut, almonds, and flour.

2 Spoon the mixture onto the baking sheet in small mounds of about 1½ tablespoons. Bake for 15 minutes, until golden. Remove from the oven, leave for 5 minutes, then carefully lift with a fish slice and transfer to a wire cooling rack.

3 Melt the chocolate in a glass bowl over a saucepan of simmering water, or in a microwave, stirring with a spatula until smooth. Using a palette knife, spread some chocolate onto the bottom of each macaroon. Place upside-down on a parchment-lined baking tray and refrigerate until the chocolate hardens.

Prepare ahead
The macaroons can be made 3 days ahead and stored in an airtight container in a cool place.

INGREDIENTS

Whites of 4 large eggs

225g (7½oz) caster sugar

1 tsp vanilla extract

125g (4oz) shredded, sweetened coconut

75g (2½oz) ground almonds

2 tbsp double zero or fine cake flour

200g (7oz) plain or dark baking chocolate, chopped

Preparation time 15 minutes
Cooking time 15 minutes
Makes 30 small cookies

BUY AND ARRANGE

Tuna tartare on cucumber slices (see p148) • spicy peanut dip (see p71) • Asian cucumber salad (see p93)

PARTNER WITH

Crispy scallops (see p24) • roasted butternut squash (see p163) • pork satay (see p109)

Cardamom-poached apricots
with mascarpone and pistachios

Ready-to-eat dried apricots, as opposed to those that need soaking, are smaller, faster to prepare, and a brighter colour.

1 Place the water, sugar, lemon juice, and cardamom seeds in a medium-sized saucepan. Bring to a boil over medium heat, reduce the heat, and simmer for 1 minute. Add the apricots. Return to the boil, then adjust the heat and simmer steadily for about 15 minutes, until the apricots have swollen and softened. Remove from the heat, scoop out the apricots with a slotted spoon, and leave to cool.

2 Carefully open up the apricots with a small knife, and fill each with a little mascarpone. Dip each into the chopped pistachios so that the nuts adhere to the mascarpone. Spread the apricots out in a single layer on a tray, and refrigerate for about 1 hour to allow the mascarpone to set. Serve chilled.

Prepare ahead
The apricots can be prepared a day ahead. Store between layers of baking parchment or greaseproof paper in an airtight container.

INGREDIENTS

300ml (10fl oz) water

150g (5oz) castor sugar

Seeds from 6 crushed cardamom pods

200g (7oz) ready-to-eat dried apricots

2 tsps lemon juice

125g (4oz) mascarpone

90g (3oz) unsalted pistachios, finely chopped

Preparation time 15 minutes, plus refrigerating
Cooking time 16 minutes
Makes 20–30 apricots

BUY AND ARRANGE

Radishes with tapenade (*see p173*) • piquillo peppers with sherry vinegar (*see p172*) • marinated olives (*see p30*)

PARTNER WITH

Yellow lentil soup (*see p44*) • spinach and yoghurt dip (*see p66*) • pan-fried halloumi salad (*see p82*)

Mini peach and raspberry crisps
with walnuts

Seek out the most fragrant, succulent peaches you can find or use other combinations, such as strawberries and rhubarb or nectarines and blueberries, in the same proportions.

1 Preheat the oven to 190°C (375°F/Gas mark 5). To peel the peaches, cut a cross under each, place in a bowl, and pour boiling water over the fruit. Leave for 2 minutes, then drain and peel. Cut into 5cm (2in) pieces.

2 In a large bowl, combine the peaches and raspberries, the caster sugar, and 60g (2oz) of the flour, gently turning to coat the fruit. Grease 8 ramekins or heatproof teacups with some butter and fill with equal quantities of the fruit mixture.

3 In a medium-sized bowl, stir together the remaining flour, the brown sugar, salt, walnuts, and lemon zest. Add the vanilla and melted butter and mix to a soft dough. Using your fingers, crumble the mixture evenly over the fruit. Bake for 35–45 minutes, or until the tops are golden brown and the fruit is cooked through. Serve warm.

Prepare ahead

The crisps may be cooked 8 hours in advance, covered, and kept at room temperature. Before serving, reheat for 10 minutes in an oven preheated to 190°C (375°F/Gas mark 5).

INGREDIENTS

6 peaches

400g (14oz) raspberries

175g (6oz) plain flour

125g (4oz) unsalted butter, melted, plus extra for greasing

30g (1oz) caster sugar

6 tbsp brown sugar

½ tsp salt

60g (2oz) chopped walnuts

1 tsp finely grated lemon zest

1 tsp vanilla extract

Preparation time 20 minutes

Cooking time 45 minutes

Makes 8 cups

BUY AND ARRANGE

Prosciutto-wrapped melon (*see p31*) • unshelled pistachios (*see p31*) • white bean dip (*see p71*)

PARTNER WITH

Three tomato salad (*see p86*) • bresaola and pear rolls (*see p188*) • creamy celery and fennel soup (*see p34*)

Quick sweets
buy and arrange ideas for quickly-created desserts

Sweets are generally served at the end of the evening and for that reason alone it makes good sense to have some simple dessert recipes in your repertoire. When the evening is in full-swing, speed and ease is everything. Choose a sweet, or two, that complements the theme of the menu, such as Mediterranean or Middle Eastern.

Middle Eastern pastries

Buy a selection of Middle Eastern pastries and sweets from your local supermarket or a specialist bakers. Arrange some authentic Turkish delight, baklava, and any other pastries on small plates. If the pastries are quite large, cut them down into bite-sized squares.

Ice cream with sweet sherry and black pepper

Take large scoops of good-quality vanilla ice cream and place them in small individual cups or glasses. Pour over 1 tablespoon of a sweet dessert sherry, such as Pedro Ximenez, then grind over some fresh black pepper. Serve with small spoons.

Brownies with raspberries or chocolate sauce and nuts

Buy some brownies or other chocolate cakes and cut them into 2.5cm (1in) squares, dust them with a little cocoa powder from a sieve and top each one with a raspberry. Alternatively, serve the small brownie squares in small bowls with some shop-bought chocolate sauce and a sprinkling of chopped walnuts.

Oranges with rose water and pomegranate seeds

Peel and slice 3 oranges and place them in a shallow serving dish. Scatter over a small handful of pomegranate seeds and top with 1 tablespoon rose water. Serve with natural or Greek yoghurt, if desired.

Caramelized grilled pineapple

Cut 1 small pineapple into thick slices and place them in a bowl. Add 3 tablespoons soft brown sugar, 1 ground star anise and 1 tablespoon butter to the bowl and mix well to ensure the pineapple is well-coated. Place under the grill and cook the fruit for about 3 minutes on each side until golden. Serve in small dishes with a scoop of good-quality vanilla ice cream.

Lemon curd spread on toasted brioche

Buy some lemon curd, chocolate hazelnut spread, and caramel sauce, such as dulce de leche. Slice a brioche loaf into pieces, toast them, then slice again into 5cm (2in) squares. Serve them with one, or a selection, of the toppings in bowls for guests to help themselves. Serve warm or at room temperature.

Fruit fools

Process 250g (8oz) of a mixture of fruit, such as raspberries, strawberries, blueberries, or mango in a food processor or blender until puréed. Transfer the fruit to a bowl and gently fold in 250g (8oz) of softly-whipped double cream. Serve the mixture in small glasses, topped with whole berries and some small biscuits.

Biscotti, mascarpone, and dessert wine

Visit your local delicatessen or supermarket to buy some Italian biscotti biscuits or a selection of colourfully-wrapped amaretti biscuits. Present the biscuits on a serving dish with a spoonful of mascapone and a glass of dessert wine, such as Vin Santo, to dip them in.

Exotic fruit salad

Chocolate mint ice cream sandwiches

Spoon 2 tablespoons of mint ice cream onto a thin chocolate biscuit and spread it out. Top with another biscuit to create a sandwich. Freeze before serving to make them easier to eat. Experiment by choosing different flavours of ice cream and biscuits.

Unpeeled lychees and freshly sliced fruit

Buy a mixture of the freshest fruit you can find, such as kiwi fruit, mango, pineapple, papaya, or watermelon. Slice them thickly, or into bite-sized chunks. Alternatively, buy some fresh lychees and serve them unpeeled in bowls.

Exotic fruit salad

Chop up a combination of exotic fruit, such as mango, melon, pineapple, or papaya into 5cm (2in) pieces. Aim for about 5 large handfuls of a mixture of fruit and place it in a bowl. Add 2 tablespoons toasted dessicated coconut and the juice of 1 lime, and toss well to coat. Serve in small bowls.

Indian sugar coated fennel seeds

Packs of sugar-coated fennel seeds can be found in Indian or Middle Eastern specialist shops, or they can be bought online (*see p223*). Serve the seeds in small bowls.

Useful recipes
sauces, salsas, chutneys, and crisps

Dill yoghurt sauce

400g (14oz) Greek or other thick, full-fat yoghurt

2 tbsp fresh dill

½ tsp each salt and pepper

Beat the yoghurt until smooth and stir in the dill, salt, and pepper.

Carrot escabeche with jalapeños

300ml (½ pint) cider vinegar

75ml (2½fl oz) water

2 tbsp vegetable oil

1 tbsp salt

1 tbsp sugar

1 tsp dried oregano

3 medium carrots, peeled and finely diced

1 jalapeño pepper or other small green chilli, thickly sliced

1 small yellow onion, finely diced

2 garlic cloves, halved

In a saucepan, heat the water vinegar, oil, salt, sugar, and oregano, and bring to a boil. Place the remaining ingredients in a large sealable container. Pour in the liquid, allow it to cool, close the lid, then refrigerate (it will keep up for to 2 weeks if refrigerated).

Fresh mint and parsley sauce

2 large handful of fresh mint leaves, finely chopped

2 tbsp finely chopped flat-leaf parlsey

1 tsp capers, finely chopped

1 anchovy, finely chopped

1 tbsp caster sugar

3 tbsp red wine vinegar

4 tbsp extra virgin olive oil

Mix all of the ingredients together in a small bowl, stirring well to combine.

Lime chilli dressing or dipping sauce

3 tbsp palm or brown sugar

½ medium red chilli, de-seeded and finely chopped

2 garlic cloves, finely chopped

1 tbsp peeled and finely chopped ginger root

125ml (4fl oz) lime juice

2 tbsp fish sauce

Crush the sugar, chilli, garlic, and ginger in a mortar and pestle until reduced to a paste. Add the lime juice and fish sauce and mix well. Alternatively, put the ingredients in a small jar and shake well to dissolve the sugar.

Mango chutney

125ml (4fl oz) white wine vinegar

90g (3oz) caster sugar

500g (1lb) ripe but firm mango flesh, cut into chunks

½ tsp fennel seeds, crushed

½ tsp curry powder

2 cardamom pods

¼ tsp cumin seeds

¼ tsp nigella seeds

½ tsp salt

½ tsp whole black peppercorns

Heat the vinegar and sugar over a low heat, stirring with a wooden spoon, until the sugar has dissolved. Add all of the remaining ingredients and stir again. Simmer for around 30 minutes, until thickened. Cool and remove the cardamom pods. Set aside until needed.

Mango mint dipping sauce

1 large mango, peeled and cut into chunks

Juice of 2 limes

1 thumb-sized red chilli, de-seeded and finely diced

Small handful of mint leaves

Small handful of fresh coriander, roughly chopped

1 tsp fish sauce

2 tbsp yoghurt

Place all of the ingredients in a food processor and blend until smooth.

Pitta crisps

6 white pitta breads

4 tbsp olive oil

1½ tsp salt

1 tsp black pepper

Preheat the oven to 180°C (350°F/Gas mark 4). Use scissors to cut the outer, curved edges off the pittas. Split each one open and then cut out large triangles of bread. Place on a large roasting tray and drizzle with the oil, tossing to coat evenly. Sprinkle with the salt and pepper and bake for 8–10 minutes, until crisp and golden brown. Allow to cool, then store in an airtight container for up to 3 days.

Pomegranate dipping sauce

60ml (2fl oz) pomegranate molasses

2 garlic cloves, crushed

¼ tsp ground cinnamon

Mango chutney

½ tsp salt

3 tbsp extra virgin olive oil

1 tsp sugar

Combine all of the ingredients together in a small bowl.

Ponzu dipping sauce

250ml (8fl oz) soy sauce

4 tbsp sugar

Juice of ½ lime

Juice of ½ lemon

1 spring onion, chopped

In a medium-sized saucepan, heat the soy sauce and sugar until the sugar dissolves. Add the lime and lemon juice and allow to cool to room temperature, then stir in the chopped onion.

Saffron lemon aioli

½ garlic clove

½ tsp salt

½ tsp crushed saffron threads

1 egg yolk

90ml (3fl oz) extra virgin olive oil

90ml (3fl oz) vegetable oil

Juice of ½ lemon

Place the garlic, salt, and saffron threads in a mortar and pestle or food processor. Crush or process to a paste, then add the egg. Slowly add the two oils with the motor running, or as you stir, then the lemon juice. The mixture should be thick and emulsified. Cover with plastic wrap and refrigerate until needed.

Sticky cucumber and peanut dipping sauce

150ml (5fl oz) rice vinegar

90g (3oz) sugar

½ tsp salt

1 small cucumber, de-seeded and finely diced

2 shallots, finely sliced

1 thumb-sized red chilli, finely chopped

1 garlic clove, chopped

3 tbsp roasted peanuts, finely crushed

2 tsp chopped fresh coriander

Place the vinegar, sugar, and salt in a medium-sized saucepan and heat, stirring until the sugar has completely dissolved. Boil for around 6–7 minutes, or until a thin syrup has formed. When the syrup has cooled, add the cucumber, shallots, chilli, garlic, peanuts, and coriander, and mix thoroughly.

Sweet chilli and coriander sauce

250ml (8fl oz) rice vinegar

175g (6oz) caster sugar

1 tsp salt

3 garlic cloves, finely chopped

3 thumb-sized fresh red chilli, de-seeded and finely chopped

3 tbsp finely chopped fresh coriander

In a medium-sized saucepan, heat the vinegar and sugar and bring to the boil. Simmer for 3 minutes, until a syrup forms. Pour into a bowl and leave to cool. Add the remaining ingredients and mix well.

Spicy peanut sauce

1 tsp vegetable oil

1 garlic clove, chopped

1 tsp crushed red chilli or chilli bean paste

60ml (2fl oz) hoisin sauce

2 tbsp smooth peanut butter

1 tsp tomato paste

1 tsp sugar

75ml (2½fl oz) coconut milk, plus extra as necessary

Heat the oil in a medium-sized saucepan until hot. Add the garlic and red chilli and stir for just 5 seconds. Add all of the

remaining ingredients and continue stirring until smooth. Add more coconut milk if the mixture is too thick.

Sweet soy and chilli dipping sauce

3 tbsp ketchap manis, or use 3 tbsp soy sauce mixed with 1 tbsp brown sugar

1 thumb-sized red chilli, de-seeded and stem removed

2 garlic cloves

2.5cm (1in) root ginger, peeled and roughly chopped

Juice of 2 limes

2 tbsp caster sugar

Place all of the ingredients in a food processor and purée until fairly smooth. The mixture may also be chopped by hand.

Sweet tomato jam

2 tbsp olive oil

2 garlic cloves, finely chopped

2 tbsp finely chopped root ginger

125ml (4fl oz) cider vinegar

1 cinnamon stick

700g (1½ pint) peeled tomatoes, chopped or puréed

4 tbsp brown sugar

1 tsp ground cumin

¼ tsp cayenne pepper

Pinch ground cloves

Place the oil in a large saucepan, add the garlic and ginger, and sauté until golden. Add the vinegar and allow the mixture to sizzle for 1–2 minutes. Pour in the remaining ingredients. Cover with a lid or splatter guard and cook for 30 minutes, until thick. Allow to cool before serving.

Tamarind and ginger dipping sauce

2 tbsp dried tamarind pulp or 150g (5oz) bottled purée

125ml (4fl oz) hot water

2 tbsp brown sugar

½ tsp ground cumin

½ tsp ground fennel

½ tsp finely grated root ginger

1 tsp lemon juice to taste

½ tsp salt

Place the tamarind pulp in a bowl and cover with the water. Leave to soak until the water cools. Mash the pulp until dissolved thoroughly in the water. Sieve the mixture, pushing all the pulp through and discarding the fibres and seeds. Add a little more water

Wasabi mayonnaise

to increase the amount, if necessary. If using the bottled purée, mix with 3 tablespoons water. Add the remaining ingredients and stir well.

Wasabi mayonnaise

2 tbsp prepared wasabi paste

1 large egg, at room temperature

1 tbsp rice vinegar

1½ tbsp soy sauce

½ tsp ground white pepper

250ml (8fl oz) groundnut oil

Place all of the ingredients except the oil in a food processor and blend together

quickly. Slowly drizzle in the oil through the feed tube until the mixture is emulsified. Transfer the mayonnaise to a bowl, cover, and refrigerate. If you are short on time, simply add the wasabi paste, rice vinegar, and soy sauce to 250g (8oz) of a good-quality mayonnaise and mix well.

Index

Useful Addresses

EXTENSIVE RANGE
www.hardtofindfoods.co.uk

This website is a virtual one-stop food shop for almost any unusual ingredients. They sell quality, well-known brands. Below are a list of the sort of foods available, grouped by cuisine.

ASIAN
Miso paste, palm sugar, rice wine vinegar, Asian noodles, ketchup manis (sweet soy sauce), five spice, star anise, tamarind, and various sweet chilli sauces.

MIDDLE EAST
Preserved lemons, harissa, olives, and pomegranate molasses.

SPANISH
Piquillo peppers, sherry vinegar, Cabernet Sauvignon vinegar, and pimenton paprika.

MEDITERRANEAN
Olives, extra virgin olive oil, nut oils, a vast range of vinegars, and pink peppercorns.

LATIN
All types of dried chillies, chipotles in adobo, tinned tomatillos, chilli powders, and salsas.

JAPANESE
www.clearspring.co.uk

A full stock of Japanese products including: miso paste, rice vinegar, soba noodles, and sesame oil.

www.mountfuji.co.uk

An extensive range of Japanese food products and sushi supplies, such as miso paste, sake, wasabi, pickled ginger, and much more.

LATIN
www.coolchile.co.uk

A comprehensive stock covering: corn tortillas, dried chillies, chipotles in adobo, fresh tomatillos, fresh chorizo, chilli powders, and excellent salsas.

MEDITERRANEAN
www.belazu.com

An excellent selection of Mediterranean olive and nut oils, vinegars, olives, preserved lemons, harissa, tapenades, and chilli jams.

SPICES AND CHILLIES
www.seasonedpioneers.co.uk

This website offers a very wide selection of freshly ground spices and whole dried chillies from all around the world. It also carries unusual Indian spices, pink peppercorns, and fresh vanilla pods. They are sold in sealed foil packets for freshness.

Acknowledgements

Author's acknowledgements

A huge thank you to the team that created this book. Thanks to Mary-Clare Jerram for commissioning and supporting my idea to make this possible; to Jenny Lane for her tireless work in project managing and editing - you are a true diplomat; and to Sara Robin, Marianne Markham, and Carole Ash for their long hours behind the scenes in design. Andrew Barron, many thanks for the lovely design and keeping your sense of humour during the photoshoots. Sian Irvine, for taking such lovely pictures. Lucy McKelvie and her assistant Fergal for preparing and styling the food.

A great gratitude goes to my husband, Patrick, and sons, Liam and Riley, for their patience while I worked many weekends and their willingness to test so many new dishes. To Jean Hanson, my sister-in-law, thanks for her flawless editing and friendship. A big thanks to Emma Leech, Marcia Barrington, Victoria Blashford-Snell, and Lorraine Wood for all your hard work and valuable input in helping me test recipes. Rosie and Eric Treuille, at Books for Cooks, thank you for your help in starting my food career and your continued support. also many thanks to Camilla Scheiderman, at Divertimenti, for your endless enthusiasm for my classes and books and to Lindy Wifflen at Ceramica Blue for the kind loan of plates and bowls.

Publisher's acknowledgements

The publisher would like to thank photographer Sian Irvine and her assistants Byll Pullman and Leo Ackah; prop stylist Clare Hunt; food stylist Lucy McKelvie and her assistants Fergal Connolly and Tanya Sadourin.
Picture credit: Lottie Davies for the author picture on the jacket.

About the author

An American self-taught cook, Jennifer started her cooking career 11 years ago in the café at London's Books for Cooks. She has a passion for teaching home cooks how to use unusual, bold flavours. She is the author of *The Well-Dressed Salad*, and co-author of *Diva Cooking – Unashamedly Glamorous Party Food*. Jennifer writes each month for *New Woman* magazine and also contributes to publications such as *Olive, The Weekend Telegraph,* and BBC's *Good Food*. She has filmed numerous television shows, appeared live on BBC's *Good Food Live,* and presented two series for Taste CFN. Books for Cooks and Divertimenti both play host to Jennifer's popular cookery classes.